GLOBAL EFFORTS TO COMBAT SMOKING

Dedicated to
N.K. Aggarwal, M.S. Grewal, and A.C. Nagi
RKG

Patricia, Stephanie, and Rachel
MAN

Global Efforts to Combat Smoking

An Economic Evaluation of Smoking Control Policies

RAJEEV K. GOEL
Illinois State University, USA

and

MICHAEL A. NELSON
University of Akron, USA

LONDON AND NEW YORK

First published 2008 by Ashgate Publishing

Reissued 2018 by Routledge
2 Park Square, Milton Park, Abingdon, Oxon OX14 4RN
605 Third Avenue, New York, NY 10017

First issued in paperback 2021

Routledge is an imprint of the Taylor & Francis Group, an informa business

A Library of Congress record exists under LC control number: 2007013153

ISBN 13: 978-0-8153-8923-1 (hbk)
ISBN 13: 978-1-3511-5740-7 (ebk)
ISBN 13: 978-1-138-35699-3 (pbk)

DOI: 10.4324/9781351157407

Contents

List of Figures and Tables

Figures

Tables

Foreword

Interest in tobacco control has increased tremendously in the past two decades. This issue has caught the attention of many parties, including policymakers, researchers across many disciplines, and the general public. This book grew out of a desire to understand the overall economics literature on tobacco and the effectiveness of tobacco control policies. However, when we started off on this endeavor we did not envision the explosive growth in the literature including the literature in related fields. We tried to make this work comprehensive but later on it seemed that the breadth of the study was somewhat compromising the depth. Hence, we tried to strike somewhat of a fine balance by including the most significant studies, while including most studies from neglected areas (for example developing nations). We would nevertheless like to apologize to researchers whose work has been inadvertently overlooked.

This book should be of interest to a number of audiences including academics, policymakers and students. Besides providing a review of the extant literature, it has new research findings (both theoretical and quantitative), evaluations of smoking-control policies and directions for future research. While most of the available information pertains to a few developed nations, we have tried to cover other parts of the world to make this work somewhat true to its title. We hope that this book will foster greater understanding of a very important area and spur future research undertakings that will further enlighten us.

We would also like to thank our various collaborators in this area, notably Badi Baltagi, Jelena Budak, and Rati Ram for educating us over the years. Comments of Frank Chaloupka on related research have been very useful. We owe a special debt to our colleague Michael Brun who proofread and commented on various chapters of the book at a very short notice. A number of research assistants helped over the years in gathering information and proof-reading the book. We would like to thank Jan Bauer, Eric Cochran, Richard Connelly, Rebecca Hodel, Ayush Pathak, (especially) Jim Saunoris, and Robert Stanford for their efforts. Goel thanks the Katie School of Insurance at Illinois State University for research support. The folks at Ashgate Publishing were very supportive throughout this undertaking. Finally, we would like to thank our universities for providing stimulating research environments and to our families for doing the same on the home front. Needless to say, this output would not have been possible without the inputs of these (and many other) folks.

Chapter 1

Overview of Global Tobacco Use and Related Policy Issues

Introduction

In recent years, there has been heightened interest among the public and policymakers regarding the costs of smoking, especially in light of the evidence on the health effects of second-hand smoke (Manning et al., 1989). Tobacco is reported to be the second major cause of death in the world. In the USA, for example, smoking related premature deaths are estimated to be about 400,000 per year and an additional 3,000 premature deaths are due to second-hand smoke. It is estimated that by the year 2030 worldwide death toll due to smoking will be around ten million annually (Mackay and Eriksen, 2002, pp. 36–37; also see Jha et al., 2006). Another disturbing statistic is that about half of the people who smoke today will eventually be killed by tobacco (Saffer and Chaloupka, 1999, http://www.who.int/tobacco/health_priority/en/print.html). Beyond this, tobacco consumption inflicts substantial indirect costs on society, including productivity losses, increased health care expenditures related to tobacco-related illnesses, fires caused by smoking, and so on.[1]

In spite of these alarming health effects, smoking across the globe remains significant. Jha et al. (2002) report that approximately 47 percent of men and 11 percent of women smoke globally, with 80 percent of all smokers residing in low- or middle-income countries. According to the United Nations (FAO, 2003, Chapter 2.2.1) tobacco leaf consumption in developing countries grew 3.1 percent annually between 1970 and 2000.[2] In contrast, consumption in developed countries declined 0.2 percent annually during the same time period. By the end of the century, consumption in developing countries constituted 70 percent of the overall market. China alone consumed 35 percent of all tobacco globally. These general trends are expected to continue over the remainder of this decade, although the growth rate in consumption in developing countries is projected to slow down (FAO, 2003, Chapter 3.2).

---

1 To our knowledge there is no comprehensive global estimate of the costs that tobacco consumption inflicts on the economy. See Mackay and Eriksen (2002), Chapter 10, for estimates for selected countries for certain categories of indirect costs associated with tobacco consumption.

2 It is estimated that households in developing nations spend as much as 10 percent of their total expenditure on tobacco products (http://www.who.int/tobacco/health_priority/en/print.html); also see Chapman and Richardson (1990).

In the last four decades governments across the world have tried to control cigarette consumption (smoking) using various measures. From 1970 to 1995, the World Health Assembly unanimously adopted 14 resolutions to control tobacco consumption (WHO, 1996). Roemer (1993, p. xi) reports that at the beginning of 1990s more than 90 countries and territories had national anti-smoking legislation. Initially these policies were driven from concerns regarding the health of smokers, while more recently the health of nonsmokers (dangers of second-hand smoke) has also been a concern. Recently, the World Health Organization has negotiated an international treaty to impose worldwide restrictions on tobacco marketing, consumption and smuggling (Framework Convention on Tobacco Control, www.who.int/mediacentre/releases/2003/prwha1/en/print.html).

In spite of all this attention, we lack an adequate global understanding of the causes of smoking and what policy initiatives are effective to control tobacco use. Are the various smoking control measures equally effective across developed and developing nations? Most of the research that has been conducted on tobacco has focused on developed countries, with the preponderance of analysis based on data from the USA. There is a crucial need for shifting focus to other countries, especially developing nations, where consumption has been on the rise.

In this book we synthesize the economics literature on the effectiveness of price and non-price policy initiatives in combating smoking.[3] While a majority of the literature deals with the USA we have incorporated comparable studies, when available, from other countries as well. This international comparison is interesting since some countries (notably Canada and New Zealand) have more restrictive smoking control policies than the USA. Our analysis is unique in that we do not merely aim to provide a summary of the literature. Rather, our main focus is to draw conclusions from the extant literature regarding the effectiveness of alternate policy measures in checking smoking and to provide directions/suggestions for extending the scope of government intervention to other tobacco products.

A Look at Global Smoking Prevalence

Demographics are an important aspect to be considered in determining the consumer behavior with regard to tobacco products. Gender, age, ethnicity, religious background and education can have an impact on smoking behavior. For example, young people are more susceptible to be influenced by tobacco advertising and might also have a different responsiveness to price changes than adults due to the habit forming nature of the product. Smoking might also be more socially acceptable in certain cultures than others.

Table 1.1 provides some demographic statistics and how cigarette smoking changed between 1965 and 2004 in the USA. We see that smoking prevalence – defined as the percentage of adults (18 years and over) that are current smokers – declined for all demographic groups during this period. For the overall adult

3 Our standard of what constitutes "effective policy" is measured in terms of the ability of a policy initiative to control smoking. We do not focus on cost-effectiveness. Ranson et al. (2000) provide an interesting comparison of the cost-effectiveness of various measures.

population, smoking prevalence was nearly cut in half, falling from 42 percent in 1965 to around 20 percent by 2004. The rate of decline was lower for women than for men, but the base of female smokers in 1965 was much lower (33 percent) compared with men (52 percent). Ethnically, smoking prevalence for whites and blacks is nearly identical, while the rate for Hispanics is lower. Not surprisingly, adults with a college education (16 years or more) have considerably lower smoking rates than the general population.

Table 1.1 Smoking prevalence in the USA

		Gender		*Ethnicity*			*Age*			*Education*	
Year	*Total*	*Male*	*Female*	*White*	*Black*	*Hispanic*	*18–24*	*25–44*	*>65*	*< 12*	*>=16*
1965	42.4	51.9	33.9	42.1	45.8	NA	45.5	51.2	17.9	NA	NA
1970	37.4	44.1	31.5	37.0	41.4	NA	38.0	44.6	16.1	37.5	28.8
1995	24.7	27.0	22.6	24.8	25.7	18.3	24.8	28.6	13.0	30.4	14.0
2000	23.3	25.7	21.0	23.7	23.2	18.6	26.8	27.0	9.7	28.2	11.5
2004	20.9	23.4	18.5	22.2	20.2	15.0	23.6	23.8	8.8	26.2	[1]

Notes: [1] Reported as 11.7% with undergraduate degree and 8.0% with graduate degree.
Source: National Health Interview Surveys (various years) as reported on the Center for Disease Control, Tobacco Information and Prevention Source website and *MMWR Weekly*, Nov. 11, 2005/54(44): 1121–1124.

Longitudinal data on smoking prevalence globally are not available. What evidence is available suggests that smoking prevalence has now peaked for males in both developed and developing countries and is expected to slowly decline in future decades. For women, a similar trend is observed in developed countries, but smoking prevalence is still increasing or at least has not fallen in several southern, central, and Eastern European countries (Mackay and Eriksen, 2002, pp. 24–27).

Smoking prevalence varies a great deal across countries and between youth and adult populations. In the next few tables we describe this diversity by summarizing how smoking prevalence varies among nations of the world according to 1) the geographic region where they are located, 2) their stage of development, and 3) by the primary religion of the country. Data on smoking rates for adults and youth, and by gender, for individual countries can be found in Appendix 1.1.

Individual countries reveal some interesting differences in smoking rates. Nearly half the adult population in Bosnia and Herzegovina, Guinea, Kenya, Mongolia, Namibia, Nauru and Yugoslavia smokes, while less than a tenth of the adult population smokes in Barbados, Libya, Rwanda and the United Arab Emirates. Further, there appear to be large differences in smoking rates between males and females in Armenia, Azerbaijan, Belarus, Cambodia, Cote D'Ivoire, Gambia, Indonesia, Kazakhstan, Lesotho, Morocco and Zambia.

International data on smoking prevalence and annual consumption by geographic region (unweighted country averages for 2001 or nearest available year) are presented in Table 1.2. The data reveal that the incidence of adult smoking is highest in Eastern

Table 1.2 Smoking trends by geographic region* (2000 or most recent year)

Region	*Adult smoking (%)* Total	Male	Female	*Teenage smoking (%)* Total	Male	Female	*Annual cigarette consumption (per person)*
Total	**27.8**	**39.8**	**15.8**	**20.5**	**23.3**	**17.8**	**1,196**
Eastern Europe & Central Asia	34.2	48.6	17.9	30.1	34.7	25.6	2,051
East Asia & Pacific	29.9	46.4	13.2	23.4	26.0	20.9	1,482
Western Europe	29.1	33.5	24.7	NA	NA	NA	1,942
South Asia	25.9	38.3	13.5	8.9	12.9	5.9	495
Latin America & Caribbean	24.9	35.5	16.6	19.4	20.9	17.8	854
Sub-Saharan Africa	24.5	35.6	10.2	17.8	19.6	16.0	344
North America	24.3	26.4	22.3	25.8	27.5	24.2	2,115

NA: not available

* Statistics are calculated as an unweighted average of all countries in the data set for each category.

Source: Authors' calculations based on data reported in Mackay and Eriksen (2002).

Europe and Central Asia, especially for males.[4] For example, nearly half of all males (48.6 percent) are smokers in this region. This is nearly double the number of male smokers in North America (Canada and the USA).

Smoking prevalence rates among women remain consistently below those for males in all geographic regions. There is considerable variation in smoking rates in females across regions, yet the pattern is quite different from males. The highest incidence of this (female smoking) is in Western Europe (24.7 percent) and in North America (22.3 percent), where the female smoking prevalence is only slightly below that of males. In contrast, smoking prevalence among women is relatively low in Asia and is lowest in Sub-Saharan Africa (10.2 percent).

Regarding teenage smoking, it is striking that the smoking rate for female teenagers exceeds that for adult women globally and in all regions except South Asia. In contrast, smoking prevalence among teenage males is considerably lower than adult males in all regions outside North America.[5]

Table 1.3 displays adult smoking prevalence by gender and level of development (World Bank classifications). As before, the data are unweighted averages for each classification. For males, smoking prevalence declines with the level of development, perhaps reflecting the influence of education on smoking behavior and the effect of public policies discussed in later chapters of this book. Less than one-third of all

4 Eastern Europe is defined here to include all former Soviet bloc countries, including Estonia, Latvia, and Poland.

5 However, caution should be exercised when viewing these data as teenage averages are calculated for a much smaller sample of countries than for adults.

Table 1.3 Smoking prevalence by stage of development (2000 or most recent year)

Stage of development	*Total*	*Male*	*Female*	*Annual cigarette consumption (per person)*
Total	**27.8**	**39.8**	**15.8**	**1,196**
High income	25.9	32.8	19.4	2,017
Upper middle income	26.9	39.6	17.9	1,453
Lower middle income	28.8	43.1	12.9	1,270
Low income	28.0	41.8	12.7	508

Notes: Countries sorted by income level based on World Bank classifications as of April 2003. All statistics are calculated as an unweighted average of all countries in the data set for each category. Smoking prevalence is in percentages and consumption is in number of cigarettes.
Source: Authors calculations based on data reported in Mackay and Eriksen (2002).

adult males are smokers in high-income countries, while that figure stands at over 40 percent in low and lower-middle-income countries.

While adult female smoking is consistently below male smoking for countries at all stages of development, it is noteworthy that smoking prevalence among women actually *increases* with development level, in contrast to men. Nearly 20 percent of all adult women smoke in high-income countries; in lower-middle-income and low-income countries it is less than 13 percent.

Overall tobacco consumption, measured here as annual cigarette consumption per person, is directly related to a country's level of development. Consumption in high-income countries is over four times the amount for low-income countries reflecting the differences in the wherewithal of the population to purchase these products.

Religious beliefs can play an important role in tobacco use. For example, certain religions such as Sikhism prohibit the use of tobacco products. Adult smoking prevalence statistics (unweighted averages) by the primary religion of the country and gender are displayed in Table 1.4. For all adults, smoking rates vary little from one classification to the next. The analysis reveals that adult smoking rates tend to be lowest in countries where Islam is the primary religion (24.5 percent). This figure, however, is only three percentage points below the global average of 27.8 percent.

Greater variation across religions is evident when the data are broken down by gender. Smoking prevalence among women in Muslim and Buddhist countries is less than half of what it is in Roman Catholic and Christian-dominated countries. Rates of smoking by adult males are correspondingly higher in the former countries.

We see that socioeconomic and demographic factors such as income, age, gender, religion, education, and so on figure critically in determining tobacco consumption. Not only are these factors variable within a nation, they are significantly different across nations. Hence, consideration of these factors is crucial in understanding tobacco demand and in evaluating the effectiveness of tobacco control policies. In this book, we will review the literature and provide some new cross-country evidence on tobacco demand and policy effectiveness, while paying due attention to these factors.

Table 1.4 Smoking prevalence by primary religion of country (2000 or most recent year)

Primary religion	*Total*	*Male*	*Female*
Total	**27.8**	**39.8**	**15.8**
Islam	24.5	39.5	9.2
Catholicism	28.7	37.0	19.5
Christianity	29.1	41.5	18.4
Buddhism	29.8	48.4	9.4
Hinduism	26.1	40.7	11.5
Other	28.3	34.7	13.6

Notes: Country classifications by primary religion based on *CIA Fact Book, 2003*. Statistics are calculated as an unweighted average of all countries in the data set for each category.

Source: Authors calculations based on data reported in Mackay and Eriksen (2002).

Tobacco Control Policies

We now turn to an overview of government policies toward tobacco. Policy makers have used both price and non-price measures to combat smoking.[6] The price measures are primarily based on reducing smoking using higher cigarette prices driven by taxes. Governments everywhere and at all levels have imposed taxes on cigarettes. More recently, in the USA and elsewhere, governments have used litigation strategies to recover costs from smoking-related illnesses, thereby driving up prices (see Chapter 9).[7]

Non-price smoking control measures include numerous initiatives including, but not limited to, cigarette advertising bans (Chapter 5), health warnings on cigarette packages (Chapter 6), territorial restrictions (such as workplace bans, restrictions on sales of tobacco products to minors, bans on smoking in public places), and so on (Chapter 7).[8] Territorial restrictions have traditionally been driven primarily from concerns about the effects of second-hand smoke.

6 A third set of measures includes programs aimed at subsidizing smoking cessation such as nicotine replacement therapy (NRT) products (World Bank, 1999, p. 53). These measures are discussed further in Chapter 8.

7 See the discussion on the Master Settlement Agreement in the USA below and the following World Health Organization website for more details: http://www.who.int/tobacco/en/atlas36.pdf.

8 An excellent earlier discussion of policies in numerous OECD countries is found in Marks (1982). While acknowledging that the policies varied considerably across countries, Marks found three policies to be common across various countries: television and radio advertising bans, publication of health warnings, and restrictions on the "creative content" of cigarette advertising.

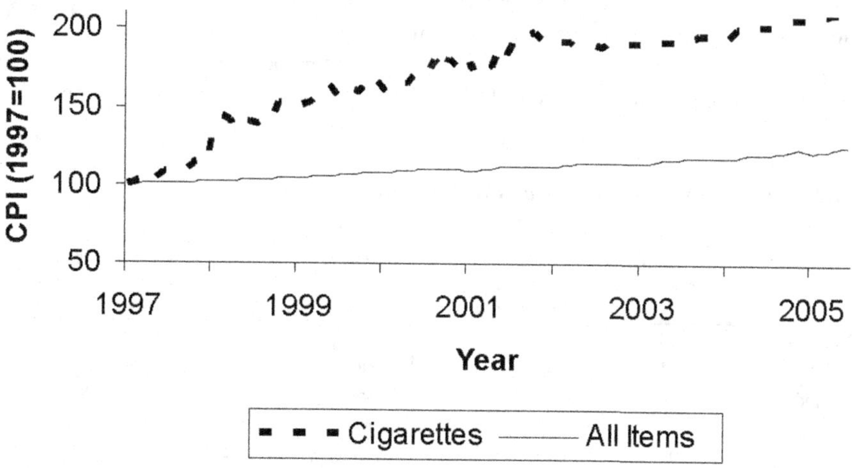

Figure 1.1 Increase in relative price of cigarettes in the US: 1997–2006
Source: Bureau of Labor Statistics

Price control policies

Figure 1.1 displays the trend in the relative price of cigarettes as measured by the Consumer Price Index (CPI) in the USA since 1997. During this period the price index for cigarettes rose nearly 110 percent in comparison with the 26 percent increase for the overall CPI.[9] The dramatic increase in tobacco prices partially reflects the fact that politicians have increasingly looked towards excise taxes on cigarettes as a means to generate additional revenues. The federal tax rate, for instance, on a pack of cigarettes in the USA increased from 24 cents to 39 cents between 1997 and 2006. At the state level, the average rate increased from 37 cents per pack to 95 cents per pack during the same time period. Beyond tax hikes, the US tobacco industry agreed to reimburse states more than US$206 billion over 25 years for their costs of treating smoking-related illnesses as part of the Master Settlement Agreement (MSA) signed in November 1998. Cigarette prices increased 45 cents per pack the day the agreement was signed. As of July 2006 the average retail price of a pack of cigarettes in the US (inclusive of federal and state excise taxes) stood at US$4.35 per pack.[10]

Internationally, Table 1.5 reports March 2001 prices for a pack of Marlboro cigarettes for a large set of developed and developing countries. Not surprisingly, cigarette prices tend to be substantially higher in developed countries, but there exists substantial variation within both groups of countries. For example, the US price of US$3.71 per pack is well below the US$6.48 price in Norway, but more than 50 percent above the price in Spain and Japan. Tax policy is an important factor

9 As of May 2006 the cigarette component of the CPI stood at 209.5, for the overall index it was 125.5 (index normalized to December 1997 = 100 in both cases).

10 Source of tax and price data: http://tobaccofreekids.org/research/factsheets/.

behind the price differences for both developed and developing countries, but other factors such as trade restrictions are also important.

Also reported in Table 1.5 is the annual average percentage change in price for Marlboro cigarettes between 1990 and 2000. These data reveal that not only

Table 1.5 International prices of Marlboro cigarettes

Country	*March 2001 (US$)*	*Annual % change 1990–2000*	*Country*	*March 2001 (US$)*	*Annual % change 1990–2000*
Norway	6.48	3.39	Kenya	1.55	-3.63
UK	6.24	5.63	Mexico	1.55	3.39
Ireland	4.47	4.02	Poland	1.51	-6.84
Denmark	4.00	-0.88	Korea	1.50	9.35
Singapore	3.92	5.45	Czech Rep.	1.42	-6.45
Hong Kong	3.85	5.23	Cameroon	1.42	-0.36
Sweden	3.75	2.46	Venezuela	1.42	1.04
Finland	3.73	2.69	South Africa	1.34	3.98
US	3.71	4.65	Gabon	1.32	-4.41
New Zealand	3.71	5.15	Bahrain	1.32	-0.58
Australia	3.46	6.70	Saudi Arabia	1.30	1.75
Canada	3.40	-0.22	Guatemala	1.29	-0.03
Austria	3.31	-0.45	Bangladesh	1.26	-1.47
Israel	3.22	2.81	India	1.24	-0.48
Uruguay	3.14	-3.76	Turkey	1.23	-3.61
France	3.13	5.15	Taiwan	1.23	-1.61
Belgium	2.93	2.80	Panama	1.20	0.69
Germany	2.81	0.00	Egypt	1.16	-8.90
Netherlands	2.80	2.52	Zimbabwe	1.15	9.00
Switzerland	2.80	2.52	Malaysia	1.13	1.55
Italy	2.70	1.78	Kuwait	1.10	-1.27
Morocco	2.63	-0.80	Paraguay	1.10	4.56
Puerto Rico	2.50	1.04	Hungary	1.09	-6.65
Japan	2.34	0.96	Thailand	1.08	-0.67
Luxembourg	2.24	3.01	Russia	0.98	-8.45
Spain	2.16	3.73	Iran	0.96	-9.00
Greece	2.05	1.21	Ivory Coast	0.92	-3.66
Jordan	2.04	-2.71	Nigeria	0.86	-2.87
Tunisia	1.96	-2.69	Pakistan	0.83	6.36
Ecuador	1.90	0.93	Costa Rica	0.75	-6.37
Portugal	1.86	-0.09	Vietnam	0.72	-9.80
Argentina	1.70	-0.41	Senegal	0.71	-1.27
Chile	1.69	1.98	Philippines	0.67	-5.11
China	1.57	-1.41	Indonesia	0.62	-2.99

Notes: Marlboro or nearest equivalent international brand.
Source: Economist Intelligence Unit as reported in Guindon, Tobin and Yach (2002).

do developing countries typically have prices well below developed countries but prices in many of these countries have even been *declining* over the decade of the nineties. Particularly noteworthy are Vietnam, Iran, and Egypt where prices declined nearly 9 percent or more annually during this time period. Given these data, it will be interesting to see how these countries respond to the recently agreed upon WHO agreement to curb tobacco use (www.who.int/mediacentre/releases/2003/prwha1/en/print.html).

Non-price tobacco control policies

Table 1.6 provides a summary of major non-price policy initiatives aimed at reducing tobacco consumption for a large set of developed and developing countries, classified by geographic region in the world. These policies pertain to the year 2000 and are classified into four categories in the table as follows:

- Advertising Restrictions (***Advt***): This refers to the degree of restriction on cigarette advertising, including such factors as bans on broadcast tobacco advertising, bans or restrictions to certain audiences and regulations, bans or limits on the location where advertisements can appear (for example billboards). ***Advt*** is an index that ranges for zero to three with a larger number implying more comprehensive restrictions.[11]
- Sales Restrictions (***Sales***): This index refers to restrictive public policy on the sale and distribution of tobacco products, including prohibition on the sale of tobacco to youth, prohibitions on the sale of tobacco products in certain locations (for example schools), restrictions of the use of vending machines to sell tobacco, among other things. ***Sales*** is an index that ranges for zero to two with a larger number implying more comprehensive restrictions.
- Territorial Restrictions (***Terr***): This index refers to territorial restrictions of some type on public smoking and/or some form of "non-smokers" rights legislation (for example designated non-smoking areas in restaurants). ***Terr*** is an index that ranges for zero to three with a larger number implying more comprehensive restrictions.
- Health Warnings (***Warn***): This index refers to government mandates on some form of warning labels on tobacco products, restrictions on tar and nicotine content of cigarettes or requirements that these amounts must be displayed on the product packaging. ***Warn*** is an index that ranges for zero to two with a larger number implying more comprehensive restrictions.

Restrictions on the advertising of tobacco products date back as far as 1965 when the UK placed a ban of cigarette advertising on television. The data summarized in the ***Advt*** column in Table 1.6 reveals that restrictions on advertising by the year 2000 were pervasive in all but low-income Sub Saharan African countries. A notable

11 See Goel and Nelson (2004) for further details on how this non-price policy index and the others that follow are constructed.

Table 1.6 Non-price measures to control tobacco consumption

Country	*Advt*	*Sales*	*Terr*	*Warn*
East Asia and Pacific				
Australia	3	1	2	2
Brunei	–	0	3	1
Cambodia	1	0	3	1
China	3	1	3	2
Fiji	3	2	2	2
Indonesia	3	1	3	2
Japan	0	2	3	1
Kiribati	0	–	2	0
Korea, South	2	2	3	1
Laos	–	2	3	1
Malaysia	3	2	3	2
Marshall Isl.	–	2	–	0
Micronesia	0	2	3	0
Mongolia	1	2	3	2
Myanmar	–	0	–	–
New Zealand	3	2	3	1
Palau	0	2	1	0
Papua New Guinea	–	2	3	2
Philippines	1	1	3	1
Samoa	–	–	2	–
Singapore	3	2	3	2
Solomon Isl.	3	2	3	2
Thailand	2	2	3	2
Tonga	3	2	3	2
Vanuatu	3	0	3	–
Vietnam	3	2	3	1
East Europe and Central Asia				
Albania	1	0	1	2
Armenia	2	0	2	2
Azerbaijan	3	1	3	–
Belarus	2	2	3	2
Bosnia/Herzegovina	3	2	3	–
Bulgaria	3	2	3	2
Croatia	3	2	3	2
Czech Republic	2	2	3	2
Estonia	3	2	3	2
Georgia	3	1	2	2
Hungary	3	2	3	2
Kazakhstan	2	0	3	–
Kyrgyzstan	3	1	3	2
Latvia	3	2	3	2
East Europe and Central Asia – Cont.				
Lithuania	3	2	3	2
Macedonia	2	1	3	2
Moldova	2	2	3	2
Poland	3	2	3	2
Romania	3	2	2	2
Russian Federation	3	2	3	2
Slovakia	3	2	3	–
Slovenia	3	2	3	2
Tajikistan	0	–	0	1
Turkey	3	2	3	–
Turkmenistan	1	–	3	1
Ukraine	3	2	3	2
Uzbekistan	3	0	2	1
Serbia and Montenegro	2	1	3	–
Latin America and the Caribbean				
Argentina	3	1	1	1
Barbados	1	0	3	0
Belize	–	1	3	0
Bolivia	3	0	3	2
Brazil	3	2	3	2
Chile	3	1	3	2
Colombia	3	1	–	2
Costa Rica	3	2	3	–
Cuba	3	2	3	–
Dominican Republic	3	2	3	2
Ecuador	3	2	3	1
El Salvador	3	0	–	1
Guatemala	3	2	3	–
Guyana	3	1	–	2
Honduras	–	1	2	–
Jamaica	0	0	1	0
Mexico	3	2	3	–
Nicaragua	3	2	3	1
Panama	3	2	–	1
Paraguay	3	2	3	1
Peru	3	2	3	1
St. Lucia	–	1	–	–
Suriname	–	2	0	1
Trinidad and Tobago	–	2	0	1
Uruguay	1	2	–	2
Venezuela	3	2	2	2

Table 1.6 cont.

Country	*Advt*	*Sales*	*Terr*	*Warn*	*Country*	*Advt*	*Sales*	*Terr*	*Warn*
Middle East and North Africa					**Sub Saharan Africa**				
Algeria	3	0	–	–	Angola	0	0	0	0
Bahrain	3	2	–	–	Benin	–	–	3	–
Cyprus	3	2	3	2	Botswana	0	1	3	1
Djibouti	–	0	–	–	Burkina Faso	1	0	1	1
Egypt	3	0	3		Burundi	0	0	0	0
Iran	3	0	3	1	Cameroon	0	0	2	1
Iraq	3	–	–	–	Cape Verde	3	0	3	1
Israel	3	1	3	–	Central African Rep.	0	0	1	0
Jordan	3	2	3	2	Chad	0	0	1	0
Kuwait	3	2	3	2	Congo	0	0	3	0
Lebanon	3	1	3	–	Cote D'Ivoire	–	–	3	–
Libya	3	0	3		Eritrea	0	0	0	0
Malta	3	2	2	1	Ethiopia	0	0	1	0
Morocco	3	1	3	–	Gabon	0	0	0	1
Oman	3	0	–	–	Gambia	0	0	3	0
Qatar	–	2	–	–	Ghana	–	1	3	–
Saudi Arabia	3	1	3	2	Guinea	1	0	3	1
Syria	3	2	3	–	Guinea-Bissau	0	0	0	0
Tunisia	3	1	3	–	Kenya	0	0	0	1
United Arab Emirates	–	0	3	–	Madagascar	0	0	0	1
Yemen	–	0	3	1	Malawi	0	0	1	0
					Mali	–	–	3	–
North America					Mauritania	0	0	0	1
Canada	3	2	3	2	Mauritius	2	1	3	1
USA	1	0	3	1	Namibia	0	0	0	1
					Niger	3	0		0
South Asia					Nigeria	2	1	3	1
Afghanistan	3	–	–	–	Rwanda	0	0	0	0
Bangladesh	–	1	3	–	Sao Tome and Principe	0	0	0	0
India	2	2	3	–	Senegal	3	1	0	1
Maldives	3	2	3	–	South Africa	3	2	3	2
Nepal	–	–	3	–	Sudan	3	1	3	–
Pakistan	3	2	3	2	Swaziland	0	0	1	0
Sri Lanka	1	2	3	–	Tanzania	0	2	2	2
					Togo	1	0	0	0
					Uganda	–	0	1	1
					Zambia	–	2	3	–
					Zimbabwe	–	1	2	–

Table 1.6 cont.

Country	*Advt*	*Sales*	*Terr*	*Warn*
Western Europe				
Andorra	–	1	3	–
Austria	3	2	3	2
Belgium	3	1	3	2
Denmark	3	1	3	–
Finland	3	2	3	2
France	3	1	3	2
Germany	2	1	3	2
Greece	1	1	3	2
Iceland	3	2	3	2
Ireland	3	2	3	2
Italy	3	2	3	2
Luxembourg	3	1	3	2
Netherlands	2	1	3	1
Norway	3	2	3	2
Portugal	3	1	3	2
Spain	1	2	3	2
Sweden	3	1	3	2
Switzerland	3	1	1	2
UK	3	2	1	2

Notes: See text for a description of the variables. '–' indicates data are not available to construct the index.
Source: Indexes based on Goel and Nelson (2004) using data from Tobacco Control Country Profiles (2003), UICC GLOBALink (http://www.globalink.org).

exception among high-income countries is Japan, which has virtually no nationally-imposed restrictions on advertising tobacco products.

Similarly, the data presented in the ***Sales*** column in Table 1.6 shows that the degree of restriction on the sales and distribution of tobacco products is positively related to a country's stage of development and regional location. Approximately one-half of the countries classified by The World Bank as low-income have no restrictive policies in place in this area. In contrast, most middle and high-income countries do have in place one or more restrictions in this area, with the USA being a notable exception.[12]

Turning next to territorial restrictions (***Terr***), the data reported in Table 1.6 reveal that over 70 percent of all countries globally have relatively comprehensive control policies–an index score of 3–as to where tobacco can be consumed. Fewer than 11 percent of the countries listed in the table have no restrictions in this area, with most of these located in Sub Saharan Africa. Whereas many countries have imposed territorial prohibitions more recently than advertising restrictions and

12 Some caution should be exercised in viewing this result; however, as the data in the table are based on nationally-imposed regulations and it may very well be that regulatory authority in this area rests with sub-national governments (as it does in the USA).

health warnings, some countries such as Singapore have had these restrictions in place since the early seventies.

Health warning labels on tobacco products date back to 1965 when the US mandated warning labels on cigarette packages with the passage of the Federal Cigarette Labeling and Advertising Act. Many other countries followed suit with the passage of similar legislation in the seventies and eighties. As of the year 2000 over 80 percent of the counties in the data set have at least some form of health warning regulations on tobacco products (***Warn*** in Table 1.6). As with the other forms of non-price measures to control tobacco consumption, the degree of regulation in this varies with the stage of development of the country and its regional location. Nearly all the countries with no health warning labeling requirements are classified by The World Bank as either low-income or lower middle income.[13]

Summary

Most governments use a combination of price and non-price measures to combat smoking. The effectiveness of any one measure or any set of measures is not clear. Are non-price measures more effective than price measures in curbing smoking? Under what circumstances should a given measure (or set of measures) be used? What are the effects of government intervention in cigarette markets on related markets? Should policies be different for population subgroups (teens vs. adults) and/or for countries at different stages of development?

A comparison of price and non-price measures is not only important for policy purposes, but it also has implications for assessing the merits of the extant literature on the effectiveness of tobacco control policies. For instance, can the effects of price measures of tobacco control be determined, as much of the literature does, without controlling for non-price measures? These issues have been identified as being particularly important in understanding the tobacco consumption behavior in developing nations (Baris et al., 2000). We will try to shed some light on these issues in later chapters. Specifically, in Chapters 2–4 we address the price based smoking control policies, whereas Chapters 5–7 deal with non-price policies. Chapter 8 addresses the issue of the success of smoking cessation initiatives, while the penultimate chapter discusses comprehensive smoking policies. These policies are compared and evaluated in the final chapter of the book.

Finally, the growth of the Internet has raised a new set of issues for policymakers in dealing with tobacco control. On the one hand, distribution of information regarding health effects of smoking has become cheaper and more efficient (although there are some equity reservations as low income populations do not have adequate access to the Internet). On the other hand, the Internet enables some consumers to bypass some government restrictions. For example, consumers can avoid paying taxes by buying cigarettes from non-taxed jurisdictions or minors may be able to purchase banned tobacco products. Thus, the Internet has the potential to undermine policy until innovations in enforcement and the legal system are able to be equally savvy.

---

13 Although some of this is likely to change with the recent Framework Convention on Tobacco Control (see Chapter 9).

While formal analyses of the effect of the Internet are in their infancy (primarily due to a lack of adequate data), we will discuss the role of the Internet under specific policies throughout the book. To our knowledge such discussion is unique to the tobacco literature.

Cigarettes and Other Tobacco Products

It is important to note the relation between cigarettes and other tobacco products. This relation is important both for analysis as well as for policy. For example, whether cigarettes and other tobacco products are substitutes or complements would have a bearing on how consumers respond to changes in prices of one good and also how public policy toward one good affects the use of other tobacco products. We deal with these issues in Chapter 3.

While most of the issues discussed in this book relate to all tobacco products including cigarettes, pipe tobacco, chewing tobacco, snuff and cigars, the primary focus is on cigarettes for two main reasons. One, cigarettes now form an overwhelming proportion of legal tobacco products. The use of cigarettes as a means of consuming tobacco is relatively recent beginning around the start of the twentieth century. Figure 1.2 shows the diffusion of cigarettes in a sample of 21 countries. Only 5 out of the 21 countries had cigarettes as at least 50 percent of total tobacco consumption in 1930, and it was not until 1970 that the same was true for all 21 countries. Two, this importance is also evident from the tax revenues generated by cigarettes. Over the 1921–99 period, about 98 percent of tobacco tax revenues generated in the USA came from cigarettes (Source: *Tax Burden on Tobacco*). In spite of the predominance of cigarettes in generating tax revenues, there remain substitute tobacco products that are unregulated or illegal (for example beedis, chewing tobacco, and so on). Some smokers shift demand to these products when higher taxes raise the price

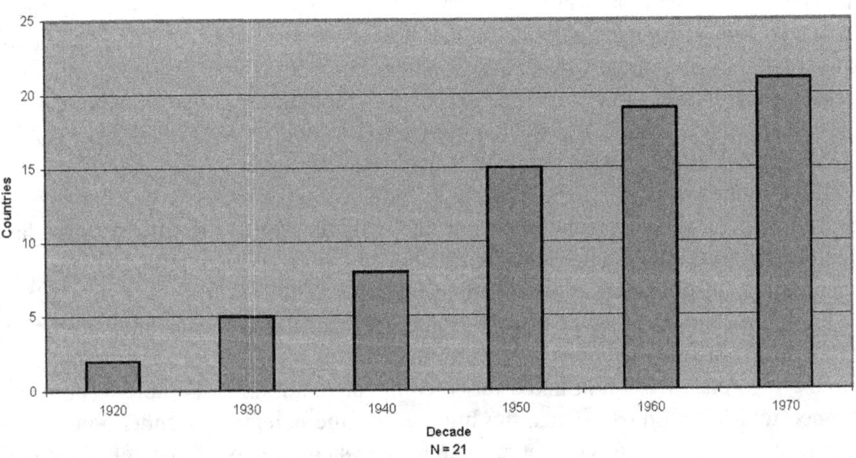

Figure 1.2 Diffusion of cigarettes (countries with cigarettes as at least 50 percent of the total tobacco use)

of cigarettes. Therefore, understanding the relation among tobacco products is important for effective policy formulation. In this book we will try to shed some light on the demand relation between cigarettes and other tobacco products.

Unique Aspects of the Book and its Potential Usefulness

This book offers several unique contributions to the related literature. Whereas there are some excellent surveys of the literature on certain aspects of tobacco demand and tobacco policies (see Chaloupka and Warner (2000) and Centers for Disease Control (2000)), comprehensive surveys analyzing a whole range of policies are relatively rare, especially those that are global in their scope. The primary aim of this book is to fill that void by analyzing the global effectiveness of a whole range of tobacco control policies.

A significant focus is on the international aspects of tobacco control, and to the extent possible, on developing nations. The attention given to developing countries is important because the available evidence shows that tobacco consumption is increasing in developing countries. More generally, our international focus will assess how the effectiveness of policy prescriptions differs across societies.

Another unique contribution to this book is that it provides theoretical background as well as empirical evidence on different aspects of tobacco demand.[14] This will not only enable readers to be familiar with the current knowledge regarding effective smoking control policies, but also empower researchers to conduct further research in the area.

There is need for a better understanding of tobacco consumption and policy effectiveness using micro-level data and incorporating the role of socio-economic policies. For developing nations, there is a paucity of tobacco studies even using aggregate data. Further, comparisons across the developed-developing divide are limited for want of consistent data. We will shed some light on this aspect using some recent data. Other contributions of this work are:

- Global public policies toward tobacco are analyzed and evaluated. Based on this analysis suggestions for government intervention are provided. This should enable better resource allocation and formulation of more effective policies.
- Influence of the Internet on effectiveness of smoking control measures is discussed. What is the impact on existing tobacco control policies of the (unregulated) spread of the Internet?
- Attention is devoted to tobacco products other than cigarettes by considering the interrelations among tobacco products. What is the change in cigarette consumption when taxes on other tobacco products change?

---

14 However, two aspects beyond the scope of current work deal with the supply side of tobacco and the health costs of tobacco use.

This book should be useful to policymakers, practitioners, lawyers, academics and students. It incorporates in depth treatment for academics, yet is written in a language that should be accessible to practitioners.

Outline of the Book

Government policies toward tobacco are analyzed in the global context in this work. These policies may be price based or non-price. Price based polices work primarily through higher taxes, while non-price policies include regulation regarding advertising, access or consumption of tobacco products. Non-price initiatives seek to alter the nature of information available to smokers and nonsmokers and to raise the indirect costs of smoking. These policies can have different effects on tobacco consumption across socio-economic groups. Every effort has been made to provide a global perspective regarding the effectiveness of smoking control measures, in spite of underlying data issues. Both theoretical background and empirical evidence have been provided on different aspects. The policy issues have been highlighted and an updated review of the literature provided along with a discussion of the challenges ahead.

The book is divided into ten chapters including introduction and conclusions. Other chapters deal with price-based policies, including own-price (for example tobacco excise taxes) and cross-price effects of other tobacco products (Chapters 2 and 3). Cross-relations of cigarettes with other products reveal the presence of demand interdependencies. Smuggling of tobacco products may be organized or casual and this undermines policy as smugglers are able to bypass tobacco restrictions. Therefore, the related issue of smuggling of tobacco products is also dealt with in a separate chapter (Chapter 4). Non-price policies such as advertising restrictions (for example media bans on advertising of tobacco products) alter the nature of information available and are discussed in Chapter 5. Other policies including health warnings (for example warning labels on cigarette packages) and territorial (geographic) smoking restrictions (for example workplace smoking restrictions) are dealt with in separate chapters (Chapters 6 and 7). Chapter 8 discusses smoking cessation initiatives and related economic aspects. Comprehensive tobacco control policies have become popular with national and supra-national governments in recent years and they are evaluated in Chapter 9. The concluding chapter (Chapter 10) summarizes the findings, compares different smoking control policies, provides policy recommendations and suggests directions for future research.

Appendix 1.1 International smoking prevalence (2001, percent)

	Adult			*Youth*		
Country	*Total*	*Male*	*Female*	*Total*	*Male*	*Female*
Albania	39.0	60.0	18.0	NA	NA	NA
Algeria	25.2	43.8	6.6	NA	NA	NA
Andorra	35.9	43.7	28.0	NA	NA	NA
Antigua and Barbuda	NA	NA	NA	13	13.8	11.8

Argentina	40.4	46.8	34.0	28.1	25.7	30.0
Armenia	32.5	64.0	1.0	NA	NA	NA
Australia	19.5	21.1	18.0	NA	NA	NA
Austria	24.5	30.0	19.0	NA	NA	NA
Azerbaijan	15.7	30.2	1.1	NA	NA	NA
Bahamas	11.5	19.0	4.0	16	20	12.6
Bahrain	14.6	23.5	5.7	NA	NA	NA
Bangladesh	38.7	53.6	23.8	NA	NA	NA
Barbados	9.0	NA	NA	16.9	15.9	17.7
Belarus	29.8	54.9	4.6	NA	NA	NA
Belgium	28.0	30.0	26.0	NA	NA	NA
Benin	37.0	NA	NA	NA	NA	NA
Bolivia	30.4	42.7	18.1	NA	NA	NA
Bosnia and Herzegovina	48.0	NA	NA	26.4	31.0	22.0
Botswana	21.0	NA	NA	NA	NA	NA
Brazil	33.8	38.2	29.3	NA	NA	NA
Brunei	27.0	40.0	14.0	NA	NA	NA
Bulgaria	36.5	49.0	23.8	NA	NA	NA
Cambodia	37.0	66.0	8.0	NA	NA	NA
Cameroon	35.7	NA	NA	NA	NA	NA
Canada	25.0	27.0	23.0	NA	NA	NA
Chad	NA	24.1	NA	NA	NA	NA
Chile	22.2	26.0	18.3	37.9	34.0	43.4
China	35.6	66.9	4.2	10.8	14.0	7.0
Colombia	22.3	23.5	21.0	NA	NA	NA
Congo, Dem.	NA	NA	5.5	NA	NA	NA
Cook Islands	28.5	40.0	17.0	NA	NA	NA
Costa Rica	17.6	28.6	6.6	20.8	20.6	21.0
Cote D’Ivoire	22.1	42.3	1.8	NA	NA	NA
Croatia	33.0	34.0	32.0	NA	NA	NA
Cuba	37.2	48.0	26.3	19.2	18.0	20.0
Cyprus	23.1	38.5	7.6	NA	NA	NA
Czech Republic	29.0	36.0	22.0	NA	NA	NA
Denmark	30.5	32.0	29.0	NA	NA	NA
Djibouti	31.1	27.5	4.7	19.3	23.8	14.5
Dominican Republic	20.7	24.3	17.1	NA	NA	NA
Ecuador	31.5	45.5	17.4	NA	NA	NA
Egypt	18.3	35.0	1.6	NA	NA	NA
El Salvador	25.0	38.0	12.0	NA	NA	NA
Estonia	32.0	44.0	20.0	NA	NA	NA
Ethiopia	15.8	NA	NA	NA	NA	NA
Fiji	20.5	24.0	17.0	15.1	19.3	10.9
Finland	23.5	27.0	20.0	NA	NA	NA
France	34.5	38.6	30.3	NA	NA	NA
Gambia	17.8	34.0	1.5	NA	NA	NA

Georgia	37.5	60.0	15.0	NA	NA	NA
Germany	35.0	39.0	31.0	NA	NA	NA
Ghana	16.0	28.4	3.5	16.8	16.2	17.3
Greece	38.0	47.0	29.0	NA	NA	NA
Grenada	NA	NA	NA	14.4	17.0	11.9
Guatemala	27.8	37.8	17.7	NA	NA	NA
Guinea	51.7	59.5	43.8	NA	NA	NA
Guyana	NA	NA	NA	15.3	21.6	11.1
Haiti	9.7	10.7	8.6	20.7	21.0	20.0
Honduras	23.5	36.0	11.0	NA	NA	NA
Hungary	35.5	44.0	27.0	NA	NA	NA
Iceland	24.0	25.0	23.0	NA	NA	NA
India	16.0	29.4	2.5	NA	NA	NA
Indonesia	31.4	59.0	3.7	variable	variable	variable
Iran	15.3	27.2	3.4	22.0	38.0	5.3
Iraq	22.5	40.0	5.0	NA	NA	NA
Ireland	31.5	32.0	31.0	NA	NA	NA
Israel	28.5	33.0	24.0	NA	NA	NA
Italy	24.9	32.4	17.3	NA	NA	NA
Jamaica	14.6	NA	NA	19.3	24.4	14.5
Japan	33.14	52.8	13.4	NA	NA	NA
Jordan	29.0	48.0	10.0	20.6	27.0	13.4
Kazakhstan	33.5	60.0	7.0	NA	NA	NA
Kenya	49.4	66.8	31.9	13.0	16.0	10.0
Kiribati	42.0	56.5	32.3	NA	NA	NA
Korea, Republic of	35.0	65.1	4.8	NA	NA	NA
Kuwait	15.6	29.6	1.5	NA	NA	NA
Kyrgyzstan	37.8	60.0	15.6	NA	NA	NA
Laos People's Dem. Rep.	38.0	41.0	15.0	NA	NA	NA
Latvia	31.0	49.0	13.0	NA	NA	NA
Lebanon	40.5	46.0	35.0	NA	NA	NA
Lesotho	19.8	38.5	1.0	NA	NA	NA
Libya	4.0	NA	NA	NA	NA	NA
Lithuania	33.5	51.0	16.0	NA	NA	NA
Luxembourg	33.0	39.0	27.0	NA	NA	NA
Macedonia	36.0	40.0	32.0	NA	NA	NA
Malawi	14.5	20.0	9.0	16.8	18.0	15.0
Malaysia	26.4	49.2	3.5	NA	NA	NA
Maldives	26.0	37.0	15.0	NA	NA	NA
Malta	23.9	33.1	14.6	NA	NA	NA
Mauritius	23.9	44.8	2.9	NA	NA	NA
Mexico	34.8	51.2	18.4	21.7	27.9	16.0
Moldova	32.0	46.0	18.0	NA	NA	NA
Mongolia	46.7	67.8	25.5	NA	NA	NA
Morocco	18.1	34.5	1.6	NA	NA	NA

Myanmar	32.9	43.5	22.3	NA	NA	NA
Namibia	50.0	65.0	35.0	NA	NA	NA
Nauru	54.0	61.0	47.0	NA	NA	NA
Nepal	38.5	48.0	29.0	7.8	12.0	6.0
Netherlands	33.0	37.0	29.0	NA	NA	NA
New Zealand	25.0	25.0	25.0	NA	NA	NA
Nigeria	8.6	15.4	1.7	NA	NA	NA
Niue	37.5	58.0	17.0	18.1	22.0	16.0
Norway	31.5	31.0	32.0	NA	NA	NA
Oman	8.5	15.5	1.5	NA	NA	NA
Pakistan	22.5	36.0	9.0	NA	NA	NA
Palau	15.1	22.3	7.9	58.5	55.0	62.0
Panama	38.0	56.0	20.0	NA	NA	NA
Papua New Guinea	37.0	46.0	28.0	NA	NA	NA
Paraguay	14.8	24.1	5.5	NA	NA	NA
Peru	28.6	41.5	15.7	19.5	22.0	15.0
Philippines	32.4	53.8	11.0	23.3	31.2	17.2
Poland	34.5	44.0	25.0	24.4	29.0	20.0
Portugal	18.7	30.2	7.1	NA	NA	NA
Qatar	18.8	37.0	0.5	NA	NA	NA
Romania	43.5	62.0	25.0	NA	NA	NA
Russian Federation	36.5	63.2	9.7	35.1	40.9	29.5
Rwanda	5.5	7.0	4.0	NA	NA	NA
Saint Vincent and Grenadines	15.0	26.4	3.5	NA	NA	NA
Samoa	23.3	33.9	12.7	NA	NA	NA
San Marino	22.5	28	17	NA	NA	NA
Sao Tome and Principe	44.1	NA	NA	NA	NA	NA
Saudi Arabia	11.5	22.0	1.0	NA	NA	NA
Senegal	4.6	NA	NA	NA	NA	NA
Seychelles	22.0	37.0	6.9	NA	NA	NA
Sierra Leone	18.5	NA	NA	NA	NA	NA
Singapore	15.0	26.9	3.1	9.1	10.5	7.5
Slovakia	42.6	55.1	30.0	NA	NA	NA
Slovenia	25.2	30.0	20.3	NA	NA	NA
South Africa	26.5	42.0	11.0	24.3	29.0	20.8
Spain	33.4	42.1	24.7	NA	NA	NA
Sri Lanka	13.7	25.7	1.7	9.9	13.7	5.8
Sudan	12.9	24.4	1.4	NA	NA	NA
Suriname	NA	NA	NA	14.3	18.5	10.1
Swaziland	13.4	24.7	2.1	NA	NA	NA
Sweden	19.0	19.0	19.0	NA	NA	NA
Switzerland	33.5	39.0	28.0	NA	NA	NA
Syria	30.3	50.6	9.9	NA	NA	NA
Tanzania	31.0	49.5	12.4	NA	NA	NA
Thailand	23.4	44.0	2.6	NA	NA	NA

Tonga	38.3	62.4	14.2	NA	NA	NA
Trinidad and Tobago	25.1	42.1	8.0	14.2	17.9	10.2
Tunisia	34.8	61.9	7.7	NA	NA	NA
Turkey	44.0	60–65	20–24	NA	NA	NA
Turkmenistan	14.0	27.0	1.0	NA	NA	NA
Tuvalu	41.0	51.0	31.0	NA	NA	NA
Uganda	34.5	52.0	17.0	NA	NA	NA
Ukraine	35.3	51.1	19.4	34.6	37.7	30.8
UAE	9.0	18.3	< 1	NA	NA	NA
UK	26.5	27.0	26.0	NA	NA	NA
USA	23.6	25.7	21.5	25.8	27.5	24.2
Uruguay	23.0	31.7	14.3	23.9	22.0	24.0
Uzbekistan	29.0	49.0	9.0	NA	NA	NA
Vanuatu	27.0	49.0	5.0	NA	NA	NA
Venezuela	40.5	41.8	39.2	14.8	15.3	13.9
Vietnam	27.1	50.7	3.5	NA	NA	NA
Yemen	44.5	60.0	29.0	NA	NA	NA
Yugoslavia	47.0	52.0	42.0	NA	NA	NA
Zambia	22.5	35.0	10.0	NA	NA	NA
Zimbabwe	17.8	34.4	1.2	18.3	19.0	17.0

Source: J. Mackay and M. Eriksen, *The Tobacco Atlas*, World Health Organization, 2002.

Chapter 2

Cigarette Demand and Price-Based Policies

Introduction

This chapter focuses on the demand for tobacco products in general and that of cigarettes in particular. Understanding of tobacco demand is important for several reasons, including determining the effectiveness of various smoking-abatement policies, ascertaining the revenue-generating potential of taxes, and for tracking changes in demand behavior over time, across gender, educational background, religion, age, and so on. Relatively speaking, given the much wider dispersion in consumer tastes relative to the characteristics and the number of suppliers, understanding of tobacco demand seems more complicated than an understanding of the supply side. These efforts have evolved slowly over time with the availability of better data (especially micro data), recognition of related influences (for example cross-price effects, and so on), and better modeling techniques. This chapter will not only summarize the literature and discuss the price/tax policies for smoking reduction, but also provide a flavor of the prominent modeling techniques. Under the price measures to control smoking, our focus is tobacco taxation.

The remainder of the chapter is organized as follows. First we note the fine distinction between tax and price elasticities and point out that this distinction can be important. However, most of the literature seems to have treated the two elasticities interchangeably. Then we will discuss the main methods for estimating cigarette (tobacco) demand and provide a summary of results from key studies. The final section will conclude.

Tax versus price elasticities of demand

The elasticity of demand for tobacco products is a key input in determining the responsiveness of demand to price/tax changes and, therefore, in determining the effectiveness of price-based policies. These elasticities are also useful in gauging the revenue-generating potential of tobacco taxes. However, there is a bit of contradiction here. While a low price/tax elasticity is conducive for generating tax revenues (as consumers are not shifting away), the same elasticity signifies diminished opportunities for inducing demand-abatement through prices. This difference has magnified policy implications in cases where the tax policymakers do not coordinate their actions with health authorities.

Generally, the economics literature has focused on the price-elasticities of tobacco products (Chaloupka and Warner, 2000), while the tax elasticities have not received adequate attention, either due to a lack of appropriate data or due to the assumption that the two are the same. However, technically speaking the two elasticities would be the same when the price responsiveness to tax (ε_p) is assumed to be unity.

Formally (denoting the price elasticity by ε_d and the tax elasticity by ε_t; p as the price, t per-unit tax and Q the quantity demanded), the price-elasticity of demand is given by:

$\varepsilon_d = (\partial Q/\partial p)(p/Q)$; and the tax elasticity by $\varepsilon_t = (\partial Q/\partial t)(t/Q)$.

Given a general demand function of the form $Q = f(p(t))$,

$$\varepsilon_t = (\partial Q/\partial t)(t/Q) = (\partial Q/\partial p)(\partial p/\partial t)(t/Q) = (\partial Q/\partial p)(p/Q)(\partial p/\partial t)(t/p) = (\varepsilon_d)(\varepsilon_p).$$

Thus, tax- and price-elasticities would be the same ($\varepsilon_d = \varepsilon_t$) when $\varepsilon_p = 1$ or the tax is fully reflected in the price. This could happen when the supply is completely inelastic. On the other hand, ε_p would be greater than one in cases where the sellers have market power and then the demand responsiveness would understate the tax responsiveness. Hence, policymakers need to be cautious in framing policies based on price and/or tax elasticities.

Let us consider a special case: assume that the demand function is separable such that the price and tax are parts of independent functions: $Q = g(p) + h(t)$. In this case, the price and tax elasticities would be separable and determined independently.

The consumers' responsiveness to changing prices might be different in the short term than in the long term. One would expect that the demand would be more price elastic in the long run as consumers are able to switch to substitutes (other tobacco products, also including self rolled cigarettes) or change their habits (smoking less frequently or quitting altogether). In the context of rational addiction models, Becker, Grossman and Murphy (1994) provide theoretical background, as well as empirical estimates, for short run and long run demand responses based on state-level pooled data for 1955–1985. The short run price response at time *t* is the response to changes in cigarette price at time t and all future unanticipated time periods. By contrast, the long run response is the change with respect to all prices, including past, current and future price changes. The authors argue that the degree of difference between short and long run responses would be greater when there is a greater degree of addiction. Becker, Grossman and Murphy (1994) found that the ratio of long-run to short-run price elasticity varied between 1.5 and 1.8. Incorporating socioeconomic variables (for example religious, ethnic background, and so on) and focusing on states in the western USA, Sung et al. (1994) they apply their framework and find the price responsiveness to be greater in the long run than in the short term.

While relatively less attention, compared with price elasticities, has been devoted to determining the income elasticity of demand of cigarette products, it can nevertheless prove useful in policy formulation. For instance, a relatively high income-elasticity would imply opportunities for lowering cigarette consumption via income tax increases. Technically, the income elasticity of demand gives the percent response in quantity demanded for every 1 percent change in income ($\varepsilon_I = (\partial Q/\partial I)(I/Q)$).

In instances where the demand is price inelastic, while relatively more responsive to income changes, income tax increases appear more appealing to policy makers in reducing consumption. However, in practice this is likely to be used sparingly, as income tax increases affect both smokers as well as nonsmokers and, moreover, affect the consumption of all goods, desirable as well as undesirable.

Tobacco tax policy

Governments across the world impose taxes on tobacco. Several reasons have been advanced in the literature as to why governments single out tobacco for special taxation, not all are related to health considerations and curbing tobacco consumption. On health grounds, such taxes may be rationalized on the basis that they internalize societal externalities (for example the adverse consequences of second-hand smoke). They may also internalize externalities to the consumer and the consumer's family (for example smokers may underestimate the risk associated with this activity) (Viscusi, 1995). Tobacco levies have also been rationalized on grounds that society simply views the consumption of tobacco as an "undesirable" activity (that is tax on sin). On grounds other than health or morality, the taxation of tobacco may represent a politically expedient vehicle to shift the tax burden onto a minority of taxpayers (Hunter and Nelson, 1990, 1992). Finally, the efficiency losses associated with tobacco taxation may be relatively low, assuming price inelastic demand for such commodities, an issue we return to below.

Figure 2.1 plots the real weighted (by sales) average state tax and the Federal tax per pack of cigarettes for the USA since 1955. At the Federal level, nominal rates remained unchanged until 1983, resulting in a steady decline in real rates. In spite of a series of nominal rate hikes since then, the real Federal rate stands over 40 percent below the level of 1955. At the state level, real rates remained relatively constant until around the time of the 1964 Surgeon General's report on smoking and health. Rates then spiked dramatically upward until the early 1970s at which point state legislatures became concerned over revenue losses from cross-state bootlegging (ACIR, 1985). It was not until the mid-eighties that states again started to raise rates in significant numbers. Today, the mean real tax rate for the 50 states stands only

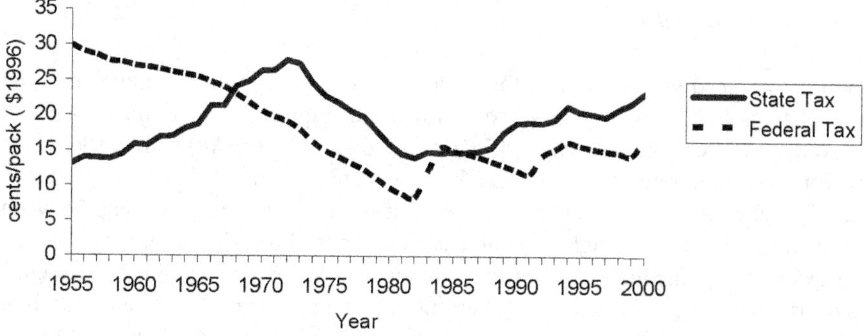

Figure 2.1 US real average state and federal tax (cents per pack in 1982–84)

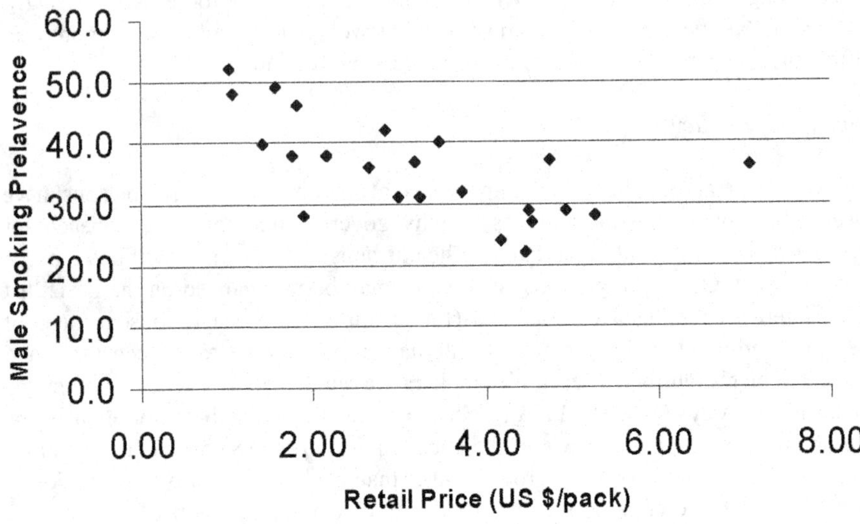

Figure 2.2 Smoking prevalence and the retail price of cigarettes, by country
Sources: CDC (2000, p. 348) and WHO Tobacco Alert, Table 3

slightly below the all-time high of the mid-seventies. It is important to point out, however, that cigarette tax rates continue to vary substantially among the individual states. As of January 1, 2006, Rhode Island levied the highest rate (US$2.46 per pack) while South Carolina had the lowest rate (seven cents per pack).

Internationally, the USA ranks toward the low end with respect to the total taxes it imposes on tobacco. For example, in a sample of 25 countries (primarily developed), the Smoking and Health Action Foundation (Canada) reports that in 1996 total taxes on a pack of cigarettes ranged from a high of US$5.23 in Norway to a low of 47 cents in South Africa. The US ranked second from the bottom on that list when based on the sum of the Federal rate and average state taxes.

Tax policy and the demand for cigarettes

Will tax-induced price increases for tobacco result in a significant reduction in the use of tobacco? Looking first at some raw data, Figure 2.2 plots male smoking prevalence (percent of males aged 15 years and older who smoke) in the early 1990s with the average retail price of a pack of cigarettes as of 1996 for 23 (primarily developed) countries. The data do not reveal a strong negative relationship between these two variables, although the simple correlation is -0.63. The country of Norway, for example, has the highest retail price for cigarettes, yet male smoking prevalence is nearly average for the sample. Before turning to a review of the literature dealing with tobacco demand, we review the main theoretical models that have been used for demand estimation.

Estimating the Demand for Cigarettes

Traditional demand models

The traditional models of estimating cigarette demand follow the framework of estimation used for other products (Houthakker and Taylor, 1970) and do not make allowance for the peculiar attributes of cigarettes in particular, or tobacco products in general. In other words, no consideration is given to the fact that tobacco products are addictive in nature, where consumption in one period affects consumption in subsequent periods. Hence these models are essentially static models where there are no cross-period linkages among the variables.

The general format of such estimation takes the form:

$$Q(t) = f(P(t), X(t), R(t)) \tag{2.1}$$

Here Q is the per capita cigarette consumption in period t, P is the per-unit price, X is a vector of shift variables including income, related prices, advertising, and so on and R is a vector of regulatory variables. The price-elasticities can then be derived from the coefficient on the P variable, income and cross-price elasticities follow from X and the effectiveness of regulatory measures can be gauged from R.

Strictly speaking, single equation models of demand assume unidirectional influences and do not focus on the supply side. The models can provide consistent estimates when the supply curve is horizontal (perfectly elastic). However, more generally, the demand and supply equations should be estimated simultaneously (Bishop and Yoo, 1985). The demand equation would be of the form outlined in (2.1), while the supply equation would include the quantity supplied as a function of price, input prices and other factors affecting supply and related taxes. The system of demand and supply equations may be estimated using various econometric techniques, including two-stage least squares (2SLS) and three-stage least squares (3SLS) (Kmenta, 1971). Bishop and Yoo (1985) find that the price elasticity of supply for cigarettes to be less than perfectly elastic, suggesting that the estimation of cigarette response should be based on estimation of a system of demand and supply equations.

These models have been estimated for tobacco demand for various countries and with different data sets. The main frontiers to be explored in this context deal with estimations involving developing countries and those using micro-level data. Also, as we have a better handle on the different institution/regulatory differences across countries and are able to effectively quantify them, a better understanding of the effectiveness of tax policies across countries can be reached.

Irrational (myopic) addiction models

The irrationality in these models stems from the fact that short-term and long run preferences of consumers are inconsistent. The addiction models are dynamic models where, given the habit-persistence nature of tobacco products, consumption in previous periods affects current consumption.[1] Another way to envision these models is to think of the dynamic stock-adjustment process associated with durable goods.

We refer to a subclass of addiction models as myopic because while the past consumption influences current consumption, no consideration is given to the future consequences of current consumption. This can be crucial in the cases of tobacco products, where current consumption could have harmful health effects in the future.

Using the notation from above, the dynamic aspects of a myopic addition model may be captured as (Houthakker and Taylor, 1970):

$$Q(t) = f(P(t), X(t), R(t), S(t)) \tag{2.2}$$

Here the new term S (t) represents the stock of habits and may be decomposed as:

$$S(t) = Q(t-1)+(1-\delta)S(t-1) \tag{2.3}$$

Where δ is the depreciation rate of habits.[2] It is because of these dynamic effects that special attention needs to be devoted to teenage smoking. If effective anti-smoking policies are able to dissuade young potential smokers, the more difficult task of having older smokers (who have formed smoking habits) quit can be avoided.

Rational addiction models

The rational addiction models are a more general class of dynamic models that improve upon the myopic models by having current consumption not only affected by past consumption, but also influencing future consumption. The idea is that rational utility-maximizing individuals incorporate the interdependence between their past, present and future consumption in their decision-making process. These models follow from the seminal work of Becker and Murphy (1988).

Here the estimated demand equation might take the following general form:

$$Q(t) = f(P(t), Q(t-1), Q(t+1), X(t), R(t), S(t)) \tag{2.4}$$

As evident from (2.4), in rational addiction models current consumption is affected by both past and future consumption.[3] In other words, in this case the discount rate for future consumption is less than infinity.

A variation of rational addiction models has been proposed by Gruber and Koszegi (2001) where they deviate from the Becker-Murphy framework by allowing

1 Another dynamic angle in some of these models involves recognition of the lag structure of advertising, where advertising affects consumption over a number of time periods (Doroodian and Seldon, 1991).

2 One interpretation why future consumption consequences are not included in myopic models is that they involve infinite discounting of the future.

3 One should, however, keep in mind the debate regarding whether consumers are really rational (McFadden, 1999).

smokers' behavior to be time-inconsistent whereby smokers have different discount rates between current time periods than between distant time periods. Using this approach, the authors find that optimal cigarette taxes should in fact be higher than the level proposed by traditional models.

A quasi-experimental method for calculating the price elasticity

The traditional method of determining the price elasticity of demand is via specifying a demand function and estimating the coefficient on the quantity (price) variable. The corresponding price-elasticity of demand can be calculated from this coefficient. An alternative approach, called the quasi-experimental method, is useful in some cases in that it does not require a formal specification of the demand relation. In practice, this method is particularly useful in calculating the price-elasticity of demand for commodities whose prices are relatively stable and they change mainly due to a change in government taxes. Two obvious candidates that fit that description are cigarettes and liquor. Even in unregulated markets, retail prices for these two commodities appear to be fairly stable.[4] Another advantage of the quasi-experimental approach is that each elasticity is computed around a well-specified time period. A pioneering application of this method is due to Lyon and Simon (1968).

The quasi-experimental method is intuitively appealing as it is an extension of the familiar midpoints formula for calculating elasticities found in basic economics text books. In particular, this method calculates the percentage change in the quantity demanded in a state where a tax change took place (called a trial state), factoring out the average percentage change in quantity demanded in states that did not have a tax change during the relevant period (referred to as comparison states) and divides the whole by the percentage change in the price in the trial state. Intuitively, quantity changes in a state following higher prices due to taxes are from two reasons: (a) the state's unique response to the price change (are consumers in the state smoking less or are they driving to neighboring (now cheaper) states to buy cigarettes?); and (b) the average of the country/region's common trends like income, preferences, and so on that are influencing all jurisdictions, including trial and comparison states (think about the effects of income tax changes that affect all states or effects of nationwide territorial restriction/advertising campaigns against smoking). Hence, by factoring out the average of common trends from the aggregate response in a trial state, we are left with the true response of the quantity demanded to tax/price changes.

The formula for calculating the quasi-experimental price elasticity of cigarette demand in the ith trial state that experiences a tax change in year t is given by:

$$\varepsilon_{it} = [((Qi,t+1 - Qi,t\text{-}1)/Qi,t\text{-}1)\sum_{j=1}^{N}((Qj,t+1 - Qj,t\text{-}1)/Qj,t\text{-}1)/N]/((Pi,t+1 - Pi,t\text{-}1)/Pi,t\text{-}1) \tag{2.5}$$

4 Even with varying prices, the quasi-experimental method can be useful when one is interested in determining the demand responsiveness to tax changes. Goel (1994) has also used this method for calculating the tax-elasticity of gasoline demand.

Here Q denotes the annual per-capital cigarette consumption (for example 20-packs per person or per adult) and P is the price per 20-pack of cigarettes. Subscript i denotes a trial state that experiences a cigarette tax change in year t and $j \neq i$ are N comparison states that did not experience a tax change in the relevant period (that is states that had no cigarette tax changes in years t-1, t, or t+1).[5] So we see that the numerator in equation (2.5) captures the percentage quantity change in a trial state, net of any (common) non-price influences on demand, while the denominator captures the percentage change in the price (driven primarily by a change in the cigarette tax).[6]

As mentioned above, this method has been used to calculate the price elasticities for several commodities. For instance, Lyon and Simon (1968) and Baltagi and Goel (1987) use it to calculate the price elasticity of cigarette demand; Simon (1966) and Baltagi and Goel (1990) determine the quasi-experimental price elasticities of liquor demand and Goel (1994) uses the method in the case of gasoline demand. All these applications are based on US data and international applications are awaited. Interestingly, the effects of inter-state cigarette smuggling can also be determined using this method by altering the comparison state subgroup (Baltagi and Goel, 1987).

Using the quasi-experimental method, Lyon and Simon (1968) calculated the price elasticities of US cigarette demand for 73 trial states over 1951–1964. They found the median price-elasticity of US cigarette demand over this period to be -0.511. Incidentally, 1964 was also the year when the US Surgeon General's report on the health effects of smoking came out. Thus, Lyon and Simon's elasticities provide a sense of demand responsiveness before government efforts to create public awareness about the ill health effects of smoking. Baltagi and Goel (1987) updated Lyon and Simon's elasticities by calculating elasticities over 1956–1983 and also corrected for the effect bootlegging of cigarettes across states. Bootlegging of cigarettes across states remains substantial. Advisory Commission on Inter-Governmental Relations (ACIR, 1977, 1985) estimated that the tax revenues lost by state and local governments due to tax evasion and bootlegging of cigarettes amounted to several hundred million dollars. Baltagi and Goel (2004) find the mean price elasticity of cigarette demand in the USA for the 1956-1997 period to be -0.4, with a median elasticity of -0.3. In an earlier study using data over 1956–1983, Baltagi and Goel (1987) find that the cigarette demand had become less price-responsive over time. Further, correcting for bootlegging implies a lower price elasticity. For instance, in the period after the publication of the Surgeon General's 1964 report and before the broadcast ban on cigarette advertising in 1971, Baltagi and Goel report that the median price elasticity of cigarette demand fell to -0.433. The corresponding elasticity for the 1956–64 period was found by Baltagi and Goel to be -0.556 and that for post-advertising ban period 1972–83 to be -0.173. In other words, whereas a 10 percent increase in the per-pack price cigarettes generated a 4.3 percent decline in cigarette consumption before 1964, a similar increase generated only a 1.7 percent

5 The year of a Federal tax change is excluded from calculations, as are the years before and after such occurrences.

6 In a standard regression setup, the non-price influences are captured by the inclusion of additional regressors such as income, advertising, and so on.

decrease in the post-1971 period (see Table 2.1). Examining year-to-year elasticities, it appears that cigarette demand was most elastic in 1973 and least responsive in 1981. A number of factors could be behind this reduced demand responsiveness over time – factors largely shrouded in data aggregation. For instance, increased health awareness among the public might have weeded out casual smokers and the remaining (relatively hardcore) smokers might be less responsive to price changes. On the other hand, changes in demographics of smokers – educational attainment, religious beliefs, ethnicity, percent of teenage smokers, and so on, might be responsible for different responsiveness over time.

Further applications of the method are limited not due to inherent methodological problems, but due to the absence of qualified commodities that are good candidates for application – namely commodities whose prices are relatively stable and change primarily in response to tax changes. Nevertheless, the quasi-experimental method is not devoid of limitations and is not meant to substitute or overtake the traditional regression method for calculating elasticities. Besides the limited number of candidate commodities, the method has the additional drawback that it does not work well when the comparison group is small or nonexistent and when a state has tax changes in two or more consecutive years.

Table 2.1 Cigarette tax elasticities

Year	*Elasticity(median)*	*Elasticity with bootlegging correction (median)*	*N*
1956	-0.52	-0.11	11
1957	0.40	0.47	2
1958	-0.42	-0.34	6
1959	-0.98	-0.81	7
1960	-0.69	-1.45	13
1961	-0.79	-0.59	5
1962	-0.64	-0.54	10
1963	-0.30	-0.20	6
1964	-0.53	-0.54	10
1965	-0.67	-0.65	7
1966	-0.34	-0.49	16
1967	-0.30	-0.23	4
1968	-0.50	-0.53	14
1969	-0.53	-0.44	7
1970	-0.38	-0.42	16
1971	-0.31	-0.14	11
1972	-0.70	-0.75	11
1973	-1.95	-1.95	2
1974	-0.30	-0.27	2
1975	-0.26	-0.28	4
1976	-0.25	-0.24	2
1978	-0.13	-0.10	4

1980	-0.03	-0.04	4
1981	0.01	0.03	2
1982	-0.09	-0.10	9
1983	0.02	-0.01	5

Notes: Elasticities computed using the quasi-experimental method. Bootlegging correction excluded all neighboring states and states with tax changes from the comparison group. Elasticities could not be computed for 1977 and 1979.
Source: Baltagi and Goel (1987, p. 751); see also Baltagi and Goel (2004).

As a practical matter, it is difficult to employ the quasi-experimental technique to discern the effects of non-price tobacco control policies, especially policies that are at the state-level and are accompanied by tax changes.

In another example of how the estimation technique could affect the results, Goel and Ram (2004) employ quantile regression methods to estimate the demand for cigarettes in the USA over the 1993–1999 period. The results show that cigarette demand to be price elastic.

Review of the related literature

A very useful meta-analysis of cigarette demand studies is provided by Gallet and List (2003). Table 2.2 summarizes the price elasticity estimates based on several leading studies in the literature using traditional estimation methodologies. Collectively, these estimates suggest that the elasticity estimates center around -0.3 to -0.4 for adults in developed countries and around -0.6 for developing countries. For the youth the elasticity estimates have a mean of about -0.6 for the 28 studies reviewed.

The simple price-consumption analysis does not control for other factors that influence tobacco consumption such as socio-economic considerations (for example income and employment status, education, religious beliefs) and the non-price public policies designed to reduce tobacco consumption discussed in earlier sections of this paper. Since the 1970s, numerous econometric and other statistical studies have been done, in varying degrees, to control for such factors and provide estimates of the price elasticity of cigarette demand. Because of space constraints and the fact that these studies have been adequately summarized elsewhere, they will not be individually reviewed here.[7] Instead, the cumulative findings/conclusions of the major studies undertaken in the last 20 years will be summarized.

7 One recent review that focuses primarily on the USA is the Centers for Disease Control (2000, Chapter 6). The individual studies summarized in that report form the basis for some of the summary data on price elasticity presented below.

Table 2.2 Price elasticity of demand for cigarettes

	Lowest estimate	*Mean estimate*	*Highest estimate*
Aggregate consumption data (22 US studies)	-0.14	-0.387	-1.12
Aggregate consumption data Developed countries (eight studies)	0	-0.330	-0.7
Developing countries (eight studies)	-0.1	-0.598	-1.0
Individual consumption data on adults (7 USA studies)	-0.25	-0.374	-0.47
Youth prevalence (16 USA studies)	0	-0.579	-1.21
Youth consumption (12 USA studies)	0	-0.608	-1.44

Source: Authors' calculations based on Tables 6.7, 6.8, and 6.9 in the Centers for Disease Control (2000) for the US studies. International calculations for the developed countries are based on Atkinson and Skeggs (1973); Witt and Pass (1981), Stavrinos (1987), Laugesen and Meads (1991), Valdes (1993), Lanoie and Leclair (1998), Goel (2004) and Yorozu and Zhou (2004). Developing countries estimates are taken from Jha and Chaloupka (2000). Also see Gallet and List (2003) and Goel and Nelson (2006).

The majority of the empirical studies have focused on the demand for cigarettes in the US and have used data on aggregate consumption, either at the state level or time series national data. These studies also vary widely in terms of 1) underlying theoretical model,[8] 2) estimation strategy, and 3) whether of not they control for non-price anti-smoking polices. With the exception of Baltagi and Goel (1987), these studies have based the consumption response on price elasticities rather than tax elasticities.

Given these methodological differences, it is perhaps not surprising that there is a considerable range in the elasticity estimates in the extant literature. The first line in Table 2.1 reports the lowest, mean, and highest elasticity estimate for 22 studies that have been done since 1985 using aggregate US data. When these studies are viewed as a whole, the price elasticity estimates range from - 0.14 to -1.12 with a mean of -0.39. Despite the wide range, over half of the studies (13 of 22) report an elasticity estimate within the range between -0.3 and -0.5. Viewed collectively, these studies suggest that tax policy is a viable strategy to reduce cigarette consumption. That being said, there is some evidence that cigarette demand is becoming more price inelastic over time. For example, two studies (Baltagi and Goel, 1987; and Tegene, 1991) estimate price/tax elasticity estimates for different points in time and report lower estimates for recent time periods. However, tax elasticities for Papua

8 Some authors have used a generalized linear model of cigarette demand, others have used Becker and Murphy's (1988) economic model of addictive behavior whereby individuals take into account future consequences of the smoking decisions they make today. Also see Becker, Grossman and Murphy (1994).

New Guinea have been found to be somewhat higher around -0.7 (Chapman and Richardson, 1990).

The second line in the table summarizes the results for eight studies of developed countries outside the USA. The mean cigarette elasticity estimate is similar in magnitude to the USA. The third line pertains to studies of developing countries. The mean price elasticity estimate for the eight studies summarized here is nearly -0.6, well above the estimate for developed countries, and consistent with economic theory (Warner, 1990). Lance et al. (2004) use micro-level data from the nineties to estimate the price elasticities of cigarette demand for China and Russia. The authors find the demand in the two nations to be quite inelastic (between 0 and -0.15). If we compare Lance et al.'s estimates to the information presented in Table 2.2, the low elasticity estimates for developed nations, developing nations and youth are all zero. This signifies that at least in some instances across these groups cigarette demand happens to be perfectly inelastic. This revelation does not bode well for policymakers trying to reduce smoking via higher cigarette excise taxes.

Several studies, especially more recent ones, have estimated price elasticity of cigarette demand using data on individuals. Individual-level data sets have several advantages over aggregated data sets, including 1) measurement problems accounting for cross-border sales and smuggling are no longer relevant, 2) the econometric problems associated with possible two-way causality between the consumption and price variables do not have to be addressed, and, 3) the researcher can obtain elasticity estimates for specific population subgroups (for example youth, low-income, ethnic groups) and estimate the effect of prices on the decision of whether or not to consume tobacco as well as the quantity consumed. However, the use of individual-level data introduces new methodological problems, including the fact that survey respondents typically under-report tobacco consumption.

In Table 2.2 the fourth line reports the mean and range of price elasticity estimates of cigarette demand of seven recent studies using US individual-level data. These studies, which vary in terms of data set, time period studied, and estimation methodology, focus on adult consumption. Despite these differences, the range in estimates is reasonably narrow, ranging from a low of -0.25 to a high of -0.47. Importantly, the mean estimate is -0.37 and is quite similar to the studies using aggregate data for the USA.

The fifth line of Table 2.2 summarizes the results of 16 studies on the influence of price on the decision to smoke by youth and young adults (smoking prevalence). All but one study report that price has a significant effect on this decision, with the mean elasticity of all studies estimated at -0.58. Even the one study by Douglas (1998) that reports a zero elasticity is only with regard to the affect of price on the decision by youth to start smoking. That same study concludes that price can significantly influence the decision to quit smoking; in particular a 10 percent increase in price is associated with a reduction in the duration of smoking by a similar percentage.

The last line of Table 2.2 considers the total effect of price on cigarette consumption by youth, including both the decision to smoke and the quantity smoked. The mean elasticity estimate, based upon 12 studies undertaken since 1980, is -0.61. This is substantially above the estimates for adults and the estimates based on aggregate data for developed countries that are reported at the top of the table. The findings confirm the widely-held view that teenagers are more responsive to the price of tobacco than adults. In short, with an increase in price, fewer youths choose to smoke, and those that do smoke less.

Having said this, it should be pointed out that a few studies, notably Chaloupka (1991) and Wasserman et al. (1991), find that price has an insignificant effect on youth consumption. The findings by Wasserman et al., in particular, are instructive because they include an index of non-price smoking restrictions in their model. When this index is excluded, the price elasticity coefficient becomes statistically significant. The authors suggest that price may serve as a proxy for a variety of anti-smoking policies and that the estimated coefficient on the price variable is subject to an upward bias when these other tobacco control policies are not properly accounted for in the empirical set up.

Chapter Summary

This chapter has shown that there has been quite a bit of research on demand estimation and how price changes affect consumption. Various methods have been used to estimate the demand for cigarettes and the estimated demand responsiveness varies somewhat according to the choice of the method. In conclusion, it is apparent that tax policy can be an effective policy to reduce tobacco consumption, particularly among the youth and in developing countries. However, given the generally inelastic demand elasticities, the opportunities to induce smoking reduction are somewhat limited. The inter-relations of cigarettes with other products might also be significant and this is addressed in Chapter 3. Further, long term cigarette demand elasticities have been shown to be larger than short term elasticities, implying that some smokers are able to respond more to higher taxes over time. These differences have important implications for the design of effective cigarette excise tax policy.

Some caution regarding this conclusion is warranted, however, because many of the empirical studies summarized above do not control for non-price approaches to tobacco control and this may lead to an assessment that overstates the relative importance of tobacco taxation strategies. This is of special concern given that such levies are regressive, with the burden falling disproportionately on the poor. Our understanding of the price/tax effects will improve as micro-level data become more accessible and there is greater focus on developing nations.

Chapter 3

Cigarette Demand and Influence of Related Products

Introduction

Cigarettes may be enjoyed jointly with other products, especially when one considers smoking to be tied to leisure. Therefore, the relation of cigarettes with other products, including other tobacco products and alcohol, has important implications for government policies trying to reduce smoking. Do consumers smoke cigarettes along with other tobacco products or in the place of other products? For example, if cigarettes are substitutes for other goods, then any decrease in smoking would be reflected as an increase in the consumption of other goods.

Historically speaking, the importance of cigarettes in the overall consumption of tobacco products (including chewing tobacco, cut tobacco, cigars and cigarettes) is relatively recent. As noted in Chapter 1, before the middle of the twentieth century cigarettes were not a major component of overall tobacco consumption in most countries (see Figure 1.2 in Chapter 1). It took nearly 50 years for cigarettes to achieve more than 50 percent market penetration in many nations, although significant differences among nations remain. For instance, Greece seems to be one of the earliest countries in switching to cigarettes, while the Netherlands stands out as one of the countries that took quite a bit of time in switching to cigarettes. This variation underscores the importance of devoting attention to a cross-country analysis for formulation and evaluation of tobacco control policies.

Table 3.1 provides information smoking prevalence, broken down by gender, between cigarettes and smokeless tobacco for the United States. It is interesting that the variation in the use of smokeless tobacco among the states is substantially more than the variation in cigarettes. For example, 7.5 percent of adults use smokeless tobacco in West Virginia compared with 0.5 percent in Connecticut. The correlation between cigarette smoking and smokeless tobacco use for men among the states is only 0.26, for women it is even lower (0.16).

In a developing country context Figure 3.1 shows that in India the prices of tobacco products increased much more sharply than did prices for liquor or wine. The increase in tobacco prices would increase the consumption of wine or liquor if the goods were substitutes and decrease the consumption of wine and liquor if tobacco products were complementary. Formally, one would need to determine the cross-price elasticities to ascertain the influence of these price changes. In other

Table 3.1 Cigarette and smokeless tobacco use, USA 1997

	Cigarette smoking (percent)			*Smokeless tobacco use (percent)*		
State	*adults*	*men*	*women*	*adults*	*men*	*women*
Alabama	24.7	28.6	21.3	4.1	7.3	1.4
Alaska	26.7	27.4	25.8	2.8	5.5	0.4
Arizona	21.1	22.1	20.2	1.6	3.3	0.1
Arkansas	28.5	32.1	25.2	5.6	10.4	1.4
California	18.4	22.4	14.5	0.7	1.4	0.1
Colorado	22.6	24	21.2	2.4	4.9	0.1
Connecticut	21.8	21.4	22.2	0.5	0.9	0.1
Delaware	26.6	29.3	24.2	0.8	1.7	0.1
Columbia	18.8	22.7	15.5	0.3	0.2	0.3
Florida	23.6	26	21.4	1.1	2.1	0.1
Georgia	22.4	25.2	19.9	3.9	6.2	1.8
Hawaii	18.6	21.4	15.8	0.2	0.5	0
Idaho	19.9	21.8	18	3.4	6.8	0.2
Illinois	23.2	25	21.6	1	1.9	0.1
Indiana	26.3	29.2	23.7	2	4	0
Iowa	23.1	25.5	20.9	2.5	5.1	0.1
Kansas	22.7	26.8	18.9	3.9	8	0.1
Kentucky	30.8	33.1	28.7	4	7.9	0.5
Louisiana	24.6	29.3	20.4	3.6	7.1	0.6
Maine	22.7	25.2	20.4	1.1	2.4	0
Maryland	20.6	21.8	19.4	0.8	1.7	0
Massachusetts	20.4	21.8	19.2	0.3	0.5	0
Michigan	26.1	29.6	22.8	1.4	2.8	0.1
Minnesota	21.8	24.1	19.8	2.3	4.7	0.2
Mississippi	23.2	28.3	18.6	4.3	8.2	1
Missouri	28.7	31.7	26	2	4.2	0.2
Montana	20.5	20.8	20.2	6	12.1	0.1
Nebraska	22.2	24.4	20.2	2.4	4.6	0.3
Nevada	27.7	25.7	29.8	1.3	2.4	0.2
New Hampshire	24.8	26	23.7	0.8	1.6	0
New Jersey	21.5	23.3	19.8	0.3	0.7	0
New Mexico	22.1	21.6	22.6	2.9	5.7	0.5
New York	23.1	25	21.5	0.4	0.9	0
North Carolina	25.8	29.7	22.3	4.1	6.4	2
North Dakota	22.2	24.3	20.3	3.8	7.7	0.3
Ohio	25.1	26.4	24	2	4.1	0.2
Oklahoma	24.6	25.2	24.1	4.2	8.6	0.3
Oregon	20.7	22.1	19.4	2.8	5.7	0.1
Pennsylvania	24.3	26.2	22.5	1.9	3.9	0.1
Rhode Island	24.2	25.6	23	0.1	0.3	0
South Carolina	23.4	29.5	17.8	2.1	3.8	0.5
South Dakota	24.3	28.1	20.8	3.4	6.6	0.3

Tennessee	26.9	27.9	26	4.4	8.2	1
Texas	22.6	28	17.5	2.8	5.6	0.3
Utah	13.7	16.1	11.5	1.9	3.8	0
Vermont	23.2	25.1	21.5	1.3	2.9	0
Virginia	24.6	26.2	23.1	2.3	4.6	0.2
Washington	23.9	25.1	22.7	2.1	4.3	0
West Virginia	27.4	27.1	27.7	7.5	15.6	0.6
Wisconsin	23.2	25.6	21	1.9	3.7	0.1
Wyoming	24	24	24.1	6.5	12.8	0.3

Source: http://www.cdc.gov/tobacco/statehi/statehi.htm

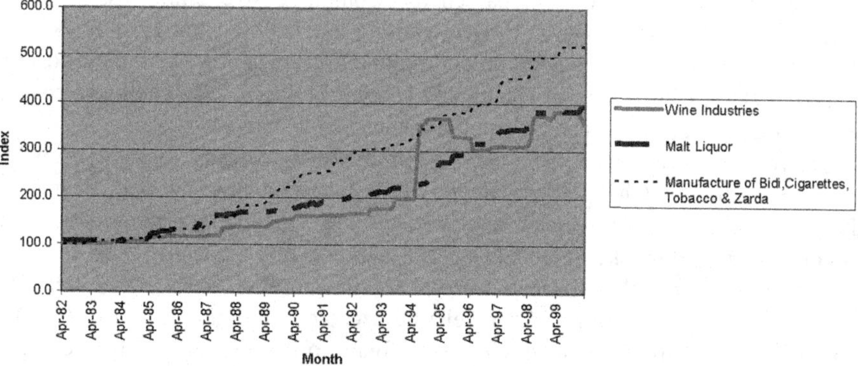

Figure 3.1 Tobacco prices versus related goods, India 1982–2000

words, cross-price elasticities of demand would tell us the responsiveness of quantity demanded to changes in prices of another good.[1]

Cigarettes and Other Tobacco Products

There is need for research on the relationship between cigarette demand and the demand for other tobacco products, including cigars, smokeless tobacco, pipe smoking, snuff, chewing tobacco, and so on. One finds considerable variation across different regions of the world, not only in the prevalence of smoking but also in the forms in which tobacco is consumed. Pipe smoking is probably the oldest form of tobacco consumption. Different variants of pipes have been prevalent in various parts of the world including clay pipes where the tobacco smoke passes through water before it is inhaled, variously called chilum or hookah (Gajalakshmi et al. 2000). Bidis, which are hand rolled cigarettes in a tobacco leaf and tied with a thread, have been prevalent across South Asia and India. Due to the slow combustibility of the wrappers, bidis must be continuously puffed to be kept alight and likely deliver a

1 Unfortunately, we do not have consumption data for the corresponding periods for India and are therefore unable to calculate the respective cross-price elasticities.

higher tar dose to the smoker than conventional cigarettes (Gajalakshmi et al., 2000). Whereas smokeless tobacco is chewed "straight up" in the USA, in South Asia consumers also take it rolled in a betel leaf (called a paan). The paan is relatively socially acceptable, especially when it is offered as an after-dinner mint.

Whereas smokeless tobacco does not directly affect nonusers, it has been tied to cancer of the mouth. If it turns out that governmental restriction on smoking is merely shifting demand to other (less regulated) tobacco products, then the social effectiveness of any government action will be undermined. Currently, there are no federal public health laws or regulations that are applicable in the case of cigars, pipe tobacco, or fine cut-tobacco in the USA (U.S. Department of Health and Human Services 2000).

The US federal government passed the Comprehensive Smokeless Tobacco Health Education Act of 1986 to place warning labels on packages of smokeless tobacco. The CDC reports that US taxes on smokeless tobacco are less than taxes on cigarettes (U.S. Department of Health and Human Services, 2000). All advertising of smokeless tobacco in electronic media in the USA is banned.

There has been some economics research on smokeless tobacco use. An interesting study by Ohsfeldt and Boyle (1997), based on 1985 US data, examines the effects of tobacco excise taxes and restrictions on cigarette consumption as well as consumption of smokeless tobacco (snuff and chewing tobacco). They find that higher taxes on smokeless tobacco decrease its consumption, while higher cigarette taxes increase the probability of smokeless tobacco consumption. In contrast, anti-smoking restrictions at the state level were found to have no effect on smokeless tobacco use. An earlier study by Ohsfeldt and Boyle (1994), using 1985 data, reports the tax elasticity of smokeless tobacco to be -0.55, and the cross-tax elasticity of smokeless tobacco with cigarettes to be around 0.4. The cross-tax elasticity suggests the substitution between cigarettes and smokeless tobacco (including snuff and chewing tobacco) and reinforces the case for a comprehensive tax policy covering all related tobacco products. These findings imply that a 10 percent increase in the price of smokeless tobacco would generate only about a 5 percent reduction in its use, while a 10 percent increase in the price of cigarettes would increase smokeless tobacco consumption by 4 percent. So we see that there could be a situation where a state government raises taxes on smokeless tobacco to curb its use and at the same time it, or the federal government, raises taxes on cigarettes. The cigarette tax increase, due to the positive cross-price elasticity with smokeless tobacco, could negate the intended effects of the state-level policy. Not only is there a lack of adequate research on the cross-effects, there is also a lack of recognition among policymakers regarding such cross-product spillovers. We were unable to find related studies dealing with other countries, but present some results for the USA from Goel and Nelson (2005).[2]

---

2 A notable exception is Chapman and Richardson's (1990) study of Papua New Guinea. While the authors do not focus directly on cross-price elasticities, they do provide interesting insights into tax elasticities of both cigarettes and non-cigarette tobacco. The results show the demand for cigarettes in Papua New Guinea to be relatively more price-inelastic (price elasticity -0.5) than that for non-cigarette tobacco (price elasticity -0.71).

Goel and Nelson (2005) used a cross-section of US states for the year 1997 to examine the interdependence between cigarette demand and the demand for smokeless tobacco. The dependent variable was the prevalence of cigarette or smokeless tobacco use. The demand relation specified the prevalence of a tobacco type as a function of own tax, tax on the other tobacco product, per capita income, and various restrictions. These restrictions included advertising restrictions, geographic restrictions, marketing restrictions and restrictions associated with minors' access to tobacco products. Thus, besides the cross-price aspect, one contribution of Goel and Nelson's work is the incorporation of numerous tobacco control restrictions. Table 3.2 presents details about the variables used, their definitions and data sources. Most of the data used come from the Centers for Disease Control and Prevention. The results (using ordinary least squares) in Table 3.3 show two sets of regressions – for adults and for youth. Given the rather small sample size, the fit of the youth equation is relatively better than that for adults. Income has a negative influence on the prevalence of cigarettes, although the effect is marginally statistically significant only in the case of youth. Taxes on both cigarettes and smokeless tobacco did not seem to have a perceptible impact on the prevalence of smoking. Thus, a cross-price relation between the two products does not seem to exist, contrary to what Ohsfeldt and associates found with earlier data. An important policy implication of this is that policy makers can continue to treat cigarettes and smokeless tobacco as separate products for policy purposes in that variation in the tax on one product would not affect the demand for the other. Of the various non-price restrictions, only limits on the age requirements for sale of tobacco products to minors seemed to check youth smoking prevalence. These results should, however, be interpreted keeping in mind that they are based on a single year's cross-section and that empirical measures of tobacco restrictions are ill-equipped to capture subtle institutional details.

Cigarettes and Alcohol

Both cigarette and alcohol taxes fall under "sin taxes" since both commodities have negative externalities. Cigarettes affect the health of smokers as well as nonsmokers via second-hand smoke. Excessive alcohol consumption is associated with cirrhosis of the liver and can have secondary effects when alcohol consumption affects the judgment of consumers leading to traffic accidents or criminal activity. Empirical evidence also needs to be brought to bear upon the relation between smoking and drinking. While casual empiricism might suggest that these products to be complements, this has not yet been conclusively proven. Further, the social attitudes toward smoking and drinking have changed over time. Over time it appears that drinking in moderation is more socially acceptable than smoking. Cross-price effects between alcohol and tobacco have profound implications for tax policy coordination (Grossman et al., 1993). However, there seems to be a lack of apparent coordination between policies dealing with alcohol and tobacco.

Table 3.2 Data definitions and sources

Variable	*Definition*	*Source*
Adult smoking prevalence	Cigarette smoking among adults aged 18 and older, 1997; Smokeless tobacco use among adults aged 18+, 1995–1996 (% of adult population)	CDC (1999)
Youth smoking prevalence	Cigarette smoking among youth, grades 9–12, 1997; Smokeless tobacco use among youth, grades 9–12, 1997 (past month) (% of youth population)	CDC (1999)
Income	per capita state income (US$)	BEA
Cigarette tax	Federal and state cigarette taxes (% of retail price)	CDC (1999)
Smokeless tax	Smokeless tobacco tax (% of cost or price)	CDC (1999)
Advertising restrictions	State imposed advertising restrictions (yes = 1; no restrictions = 0)	CDC (1999)
Indoor restrictions	State-level indoor smoke free restrictions on government worksites, private worksites, restaurants, day care centers, home-based day care (Range: 0–5; with 0 = no restrictions.)	CDC (1999)
Minor access	Restrictions for minors to purchase, possess, use tobacco products. Restrictions on vending machines, signage, licensure (Range: 0–6; with 0 = no restrictions)	CDC (1999)
Age limits	Minimum age for sale of tobacco to minors (years)	CDC (1999)

Note: BEA is Bureau of Economic Analysis; CDC is Centers for Disease Control and Prevention.
Source: Goel and Nelson (2005).

Table 3.3 Interdependence between US cigarettes and smokeless tobacco demand. Dependent variable: percentage of smokers, 1997

	Adults	*Youth*
Constant	27.67*(8.78)	436.95*(3.65)
Income	−0.00003 (0.22)	-0.0005#(1.82)
Cigarette tax	−0.09 (0.99)	−0.05 (0.24)
Smokeless tax	−0.009 (0.30)	0.06 (0.78)
Advertising restrictions	0.79 (0.79)	0.09 (0.03)
Indoor restrictions	−0.30 (0.88)	−1.02 (1.08)
Minor access		0.49 (0.59)
Age limits		-21.45*(3.26)
N	49	33
Adj. -R^2	0.06	0.29
F	1.60	2.86*

Note: t-statistics are in parentheses. *denotes statistical significance at least at the 5% level.
# denotes statistical significance at least at the 10% level.
Source: Goel and Nelson (2005).

Goel and Morey's (1995) study of US states using annual data over 1959–82 estimated cross-price elasticities between cigarettes and liquor using a relation of the following general form:

$$Qi = f(Pi, Pj, I, ADVi, REGi) \tag{3.1}$$

$$i \neq j;\ i, j = \text{cigarettes, liquor}$$

Here Q is per capita consumption in a state in a year

P = price per unit
I = per capita disposable income
ADV = advertising spending
REG = dummy variable for regulation

In the regression following (3.1) the coefficient on Pi would give the own-price elasticity of demand (expected to be negative), that on Pj would give the cross-price elasticity of demand[3] (positive or negative depending upon whether the goods are substitutes or complements) and that on I would give the income elasticity of demand (expected to be positive). The effect of advertising is generally expected to be positive, unless advertising is ineffective or is accompanied by consumption reducing messages, and the coefficient on regulation would be negative if regulation is effective in checking consumption.

Goel and Morey found cigarettes and liquor to be substitutes implying that higher liquor taxes would result in greater cigarette consumption. Such relation holds even when the authors control for the effects of regulatory changes, such as the 1971 broadcast ban on cigarette advertising. The cross-price elasticities between cigarettes and liquor are found to lie between 0.1 and 0.35. The state-level aggregation in Goel and Morey's US data masks any role age, gender, and other socio-economic factors might play. On the other hand, the positive cross-price elasticities make sense when one considers the relation of cigarettes and liquor with leisure. If consumers view cigarette and liquor consumption as complementary to leisure, then these two products might very well be substitute to each other. Dee (1999) tried to examine the cross effects between smoking and drinking using survey data on teenagers. The main finding of this study is that for teenagers drinking and smoking are "highly complementary" (p. 791). Complementarity between smoking and alcohol was also found in the case of Canada (Gruber et al., 2003). More attention needs to be paid

3 The elasticities would follow directly from the model if the variables are in natural logarithms or could be calculated indirectly if they are not. Referring back to the demand specifications discussed in Chapter 2, studies examining cross-price elasticities of cigarettes with other products would include the price of the related good as an additional regressor. Then the cross-price elasticity is derived from the resulting coefficient as $\varepsilon xy = (\partial Qx/\partial Py)(Py/Qx)$, where Q and P denote quantity and price, respectively; x denotes cigarettes and y the related good such as smokeless tobacco or alcohol.

toward understanding the relation of cigarettes with other products, especially in a cross-country context.

Chapter Summary

In this chapter, we have focused on the cross-effects between cigarettes and other products. Determination of these effects is important to ascertain spillovers from policy actions. Formal estimation of these effects is still in its infancy in the literature and more research is needed. Nevertheless, we present some recent results of attempts to determine the cross-demand relation between cigarettes and smokeless tobacco. The results show that the demands for the two products do not seem to be related, although the evidence in support of this proposition is somewhat limited. Whereas the literature has focused a little in recent years on the cross-price effects, interesting directions would involve examination of cross-advertising and cross-regulatory effects. Does cigarette advertising increase or decrease the consumption of liquor? Whereas researchers are slowly beginning to recognize that cigarette demand might be sensitive to prices of related products, it does not seem that such realization has yet dawned on policymakers.

Chapter 4

Tobacco Smuggling

Introduction

This chapter considers the issue of smuggling of tobacco products in general and cigarettes in particular. Due to the relatively long shelf life of tobacco products and relative ease of transportation, smuggling is an important problem facing policymakers. Not only are any restrictions limiting the quantity of tobacco sold bypassed with the help of smuggling, there is also substantial loss of tax revenue to governments. Further, the smuggling of tobacco has both intra-national and international aspects. Regulatory differences, including price and non-price differentials, across jurisdictions give rise to smuggling both across regions within a country and across international borders. However, as we discuss below, not all forms of tobacco smuggling are illegal. For instance, purchases by tourists to avoid higher taxes at home remain legal in most cases.

The International Union against Cancer (UICC) notes that for many years globally a discrepancy between cigarette exports and imports has persisted, where exports have substantially exceeded imports (http://globalink.org/). Given the longevity of this difference, the only plausible explanation seems to be a persistent smuggling of cigarettes, with the cigarette manufacturers being the primary beneficiaries.

Smuggling poses obvious problems for regulators trying to raise tax revenues and/or curb smoking. Such activity also makes matters difficult for researchers trying to understand the demand responsiveness (a.k.a. price elasticities) in a region.[1] Whether some region imports or exports cigarettes illegally via bootlegging, its demand responsiveness is likely to be affected by changing/different prices in other regions. For instance, when a state/country raises cigarette taxes, importing/smuggling cigarettes from now relatively cheaper neighboring regions becomes attractive.[2]

There is substantial research on cigarette smuggling in the case of USA regarding how bootlegging of cigarettes takes place across states and neighboring countries. However, evidence on other countries, especially formal research, is scarce. In this chapter we will review the existing literature, provide some theoretical and empirical

1 The seminal theoretical work on the economics of smuggling is due to Bhagwati and Hansen (1973).

2 However, not all cigarette smuggling is necessarily bad. Thursby et al. (1991) argue that smuggling could be welfare enhancing when smuggled cigarettes are indistinguishable from legal cigarettes and this puts a downward pressure on the price.

analyses of smuggling, discuss policy issues and suggest directions for future research. An overview of global smoking activity is provided in the appendix.

Tobacco smuggling can take various forms. Joossens et al. (2000) classify the smuggling of cigarettes into three categories:

- *Legal smuggling*: This type of smuggling includes cross-border shopping by residents living close to the border (ACIR (1977, 1985); Warner (1982), Baltagi and Levin (1986), Fox (1986), Baltagi and Goel (1987), Hunter and Nelson (1992), Becker, Grossman and Murphy (1994), Coates (1995), and Nelson (2002)); shopping by tourists (Merriman, Yurekli and Chaloupka, 2000); and duty-free sales at international ports. For instance, consumers from high tax states (Massachusetts) drive to neighboring states (New Hampshire) to buy cheaper cigarettes. Smuggling can also take place at military bases and Indian reservations because both are exempt from state taxes.
- *Quasi-legal smuggling*: Smuggling of this nature includes sales over the Internet, where the legal issues have still not been clarified regarding who has the jurisdiction over tax collections. There is also the feasibility issue concerning the practicality of taxing Internet sales. Also, included in this category are gray market sales of cigarettes. For instance, certain countries have export-promotion zones where businesses are subsidized but the goods produced are meant for export. Cigarettes produced in such zones might be directed toward the domestic market.
- *Illegal smuggling*: Cigarette sales in this category include bootlegging and organized smuggling of cigarettes over different jurisdictions (ACIR (1977, 1985), Baltagi and Levin (1986), Baltagi and Goel (1987), Thursby and Thursby (2000)). Illegal smuggling might be undertaken by traders themselves or by organized criminals.

A Theoretical Model of Cigarette Smuggling

Before proceeding to a discussion of the evidence regarding tobacco smuggling activities and the effectiveness of related policy measures, it is useful to spend some time on the underlying theoretical framework that would explain smuggling activities. Here we outline a simple theoretical model of smuggling given by Norton (1988). We also incorporate a simple extension of this model from Merriman, Yurekli and Chaloupka (2000) and propose and analyze an extension of our own. The country into which goods (cigarettes) are smuggled is called Home. Its trading partner country is referred to as Abroad. A firm is located at a distance d from Home. The trader's holdings of the good are fixed at a point in time in this static analysis. This is not too restrictive an assumption when one thinks of agricultural products or of goods with long gestation periods in production. The firm must choose between domestic sales and exports. Exports preclude sales at the market price abroad. Also, exports could be in the form of legal sales, smuggled goods or some combination of the two. Both smuggled and legal goods face some loss in transportation. Norton assumes that trading in the Abroad market yields the firm zero economic profits. An ad valorem tax of t percent is imposed on Home sales. In the case of smuggling, there is some probability of detection, upon which the smuggled goods are subject to a fine. The firm chooses its legal and illegal sales to maximize profits. A detailed description of the variables used in the model follows:

Q = quantity (fixed) available to the trader
p = price Abroad
t = ad valorem tax, payable by exporter on Home sales
$[p\,(1+t)+\theta]$: market price throughout Home

θ is assumed to be small relative to p and it could be positive, negative or zero, depending upon how much of the tax is passed to the consumer. One could also think about θ as capturing the higher price that consumers might have to pay for regulations (for example higher cigarette prices due to restrictions on sales to minors).

qs = quantity of cigarettes smuggled
qL = quantity legally exported by the firm
$s(d)$, $L(d)$ = The fractions of smuggled and legally exported goods, respectively, transported over distance d, that perish/evaporate in transit; such that $0 < s,\ L < 1$. L may also be interpreted as non-price restrictions on legal cigarette sales (for example bans on sales to minor) and s may be the costs imposed on bootlegged cigarettes as a result of any such action.

$(1\text{-}\mu)$ = probability of smoking detection. It is assumed that greater legal sales help camouflage smuggling, while greater smuggling, for the same amount of legal sales, makes smuggling easier to detect. Formally, $\mu = \mu\,(qs, qL)$; $0 < \mu < 1$; and $(\partial\mu/\partial\, s) \equiv \mu_s < 0$ $(\partial\mu/\partial \mathrm{L}) \equiv \mu_L > 0$. Merriman, Yurekli and Chaloupka (2000) allow the probability of detection to be dependent on the stringency of enforcement, k, such that $\mu_k < 0$; and $\mu_{ks} = \mu_{kL} = 0$.

α = share of sales from detected smuggled goods that are charged as a penalty

Given this structure, we consider alternate scenarios where first smuggling is riskless and then smuggled goods face the possibility of detection and penalty.

Riskless smuggling

If smuggling were riskless, given distance d, the firm chooses the amount of smuggled and legal shipments to maximize the net profit from smuggled and legal sales. All this is subject to the constraint that the total amount available for any kind of sale is fixed at Q. Formally, the objective of the firm can be shown as:

$$\max_{qs,\, qL} \pi(d) = (p + pt + \theta)\,(1\text{-}s)\,qs + (p + \theta)(1\text{-}L)\,qL\text{-}p\,(qs + qL) \tag{4.1}$$

subject to $qs + qL \le \mathrm{Q}$

$qs, qL \geq 0$

The first term in (4.1) is revenues from smuggled sales, the second term is legal sales revenues and the final term shows the revenues from sales abroad (which are assumed to earn zero economic profits). The corresponding Kuhn-Tucker conditions can be solved by setting up the Lagrangean and comparative-static effects analyzed (see Norton, 1988, pp. 110–111, for details). We turn next to the more interesting (and more realistic) case where smuggling is risky.

Risky smuggling

In this case cigarette smuggling is risky in that there is some chance of the smuggled goods being caught by the law enforcement authorities, such as the Bureau of Alcohol, Tobacco and Firearms in the USA. The objective of the firm facing a probability $(1\text{-}\mu)$ of smuggling detection becomes:

$$\max_{qs,\, qL} \pi(d) = \mu(qs, qL)\,(p + pt + \theta)\,(1\text{-}s)\,qs - (1\text{-}\mu)\alpha(1\text{-}s)\,pqs + (p + \theta)(1\text{-}L)\,qL - p\,(qs + qL) \tag{4.2}$$

subject to $qs + qL \leq Q$; $qs, qL \geq 0$

The term $(1\text{-}\mu)\alpha(1\text{-}s)\,pqs$ captures the penalty in case the smuggle shipment is intercepted by the authorities.

The Lagrangean for (4.2) is:

$$\text{L} = \pi + \lambda(Q - qs - qL) \tag{4.3}$$

Here λ is the Lagrangean multiplier. The corresponding Kuhn-Tucker conditions are:

$$(\partial L/\partial qs) \leq 0 \Rightarrow (p{+}pt{+}p\,\alpha{+}\theta)(1\text{-}s)qs\,\mu_s + \mu(p + pt + \theta)\,(1\text{-}s) - (1\text{-}\mu)\,\alpha\,(1\text{-}s)\,p - p \leq \lambda \tag{4.4a}$$

$$(\partial L/\partial \text{q}L) \leq 0 \Rightarrow (p + pt + p\,\alpha + \theta)\,(1\text{-}s)\,qs\,\mu_L + \theta\text{-}pL\text{-}\theta L \leq \lambda \tag{4.4b}$$

$$(\partial L/\partial \lambda) \leq 0 \Rightarrow Q - qs - qL \geq 0 \tag{4.4c}$$

Assuming interior solutions, where the constraints are strictly binding, we denote the following notation:

$$\text{A} \equiv (p + pt + p\,\alpha + \theta)\,(1\text{-}s) > 0$$
$$\text{B} \equiv -p - p\,\alpha(1\text{-}s) < 0$$
$$\text{C} \equiv \theta\text{-}pL\text{-}\theta L$$

From (4.4a) And (4.4b) one can solve for qs as:

$$qs = (C - B - A\mu) / A(\mu_s - \mu_L) \tag{4.5}$$

qs denotes the profit-maximizing level of smuggling, considering the risk of detection. The advantage of this simple model is that it yields a closed form solution. One can now evaluate how the profit-maximizing smuggling would change when the parameters of the model change. For instance, the effects of four policy variables can be evaluated: penalty (α), tax (t), enforcement (k) and regulation (L). We turn to an evaluation of these next.

Effect of higher taxes

The government might raise cigarette taxes to raise revenues and/or to curb smoking. These objectives are undermined when such tax increases raise smuggling. We can test the effect of taxes by taking the partial derivative of (4.5) with respect to *t*

$$(\partial qs/\partial t) = (-Cp + Bp) / A(\mu_s - \mu_L) > 0 \tag{4.6}$$

Note $\mu_s < 0$ and $\mu_L > 0$. Thus, higher cigarette taxes lead to greater smuggling—a result in accord with our intuition (see Norton, 1988).

Effect of greater punishment

Higher smuggling penalties (α) upon being caught might deter smuggling. On the other hand, a lighter sentence would fail to act as a deterrent to smuggling. Formally,

$$(\partial qs/\partial \alpha) = [p(1-s) / A(\mu_s - \mu_L)][-qsA(\mu_s - \mu_L) + A(\mu - 1)] < 0 \tag{4.7}$$

recall $\mu < 1$

Greater penalties lower smuggling (Norton, 1988).

Effect of greater enforcement

Greater enforcement might mean more personnel devoted to apprehension of smuggling activities or better policing mechanisms. Norton's basic model was extended by Merriman, Yurekli and Chaloupka (2000) by having the probability of being caught be dependent on the level of enforcement, that is μ(k). The effect of greater enforcement is given by

$$(\partial qs/\partial k) = -\mu_k / (\mu_s - \mu_L) < 0 \tag{4.8}$$

using $\mu_s < 0$; $\mu_L > 0$; $\mu_{sk} = \mu_{Lk} = 0$

Higher enforcement also has an effect similar to a greater penalty in that both reduce the degree of smuggling.

Effect of greater non-price restrictions on legal cigarette sales

We add another twist to the analysis by determining an effect of a change in non-price strategies. These strategies might be restrictions that deter free sale of tobacco products (for example bans on vending machine sales, bans on sales to minors, and so on). A change in non-price strategies such that legal cigarettes are harder to obtain and/or consume, would make smuggled cigarettes more attractive to potential smokers. For instance, when restrictions on cigarette sales to minors are imposed or strengthened, minors might resort to buying smuggled cigarettes. Formally,

$$(\partial qs/\partial L) = \{[A(\mu_s - \mu_L)][-p - \theta] - (C - B - A\mu)A(\mu_{sL} - \mu_{LL})\} / [A(\mu_s - \mu_L)]^2 \qquad (4.9)$$

Ignoring the second-order terms (that is $\mu_{sL} = \mu_{LL} = 0$), the effect of greater non-price restrictions would be similar to higher taxes and both would spur smuggling. Hence, policy coordination is important to achieve effective results. For instance, in the absence of policy coordination, there could be situations where higher taxes induce smuggling, while lower restrictions make it less attractive. Alternately, greater enforcement might deter smuggling, but low penalties might make it attractive.

In closing this section, we propose some extensions to Norton's model. One extension would be to include competition in the marketplace. What role do strategic considerations play in the firm's choice to smuggle? Thursby et al. (1991) have made some headway in this direction. Another extension might be to include dynamic considerations. For instance: how do smuggling penalties differ for first-time offenders from repeat offenders?

Cigarette Smuggling in the USA

Since there is a substantial amount of information on smuggling in the USA, we turn to its discussion first. Smuggling of cigarettes across states is significant in the USA. Overall, Fleenor (1998) estimated that 13.3 percent of the cigarette market share was accounted for by all categories of cross-border activity.[3] This figure is higher than the three to four percent market share that Thursby and Thursby (2000) estimated for the seventies, but their analysis is restricted to the illegally smuggled cigarettes (what they refer to as "commercial smuggling") category noted above.

A major factor driving bootlegging activity in the USA is differences in cigarette tax rates across the states. For example, as of January 2006 the state tax rate (excluding local taxes) ranged from US$2.46 per pack in Rhode Island to seven cents in South Carolina (Federation of Tax Administrators). Fleenor (1998) estimated that four states (Hawaii, New York, Washington, and Michigan) and the District of Columbia lost 30 percent or more of their tax base to cross-border activity in 1997. In contrast, states with large "exports" of cigarettes included Kentucky, New Hampshire, and Indiana. All of these states had relatively low tax rates on cigarettes,

3 Cross-border activity is defined here to include all three categories of smuggling discussed above.

at least within the region where they are located.[4] The considerable variance across states in smuggling activity has been documented by others, including the ACIR (1977, 1985); Saba et al. (1995), and Thursby and Thursby (2000).

It has also been shown that smuggling trends over time follow the magnitude of these tax differentials among the states (ACIR, 1985; Fleenor 1998; and Thursby and Thursby, 2000). For example, Fleenor (1998) estimates the market share of cross-border activity increased from 5.4 percent in 1982 – a period when interstate tax differentials were relatively low – to 13.3 percent in 1997, reflecting the widening disparity among state cigarette tax rates that began around 1983.

To gain further insight on the influence of interstate cigarette tax differentials on smuggling activity Baltagi and Levin (1986) examined state-level US data for 46 states over the years 1963–80. They employed "standard" regression techniques, accounting for the bootlegging effect by including the lowest cigarette price of all neighbors of a state as an additional regressor. A positive and statistically significant coefficient on the neighboring price variable signified bootlegging was significant as the state in question was attracting outside buyers when its neighbor raised its cigarette price. Baltagi and Levin (1986) did find the neighbor price coefficient to be positive and significant. The aggregation in Baltagi and Levin's treatment of the neighboring price failed to account for the fact that in large states, only residents close to the borders with other states were influenced by different prices and populations farther away from the border were unlikely to respond, given the relatively large transactions costs (think Texas, Ohio, and Florida).

Thursby et al. (1991) try to distinguish between the effects of casual and organized smuggling of cigarettes. Casual smuggling takes place when individuals take merchandise across jurisdictions for their personal use, while organized smuggling involved goods transported across several jurisdictions for the purpose of sale to others. The neighboring price is used as a proxy for the effects of casual smuggling and the effect of organized smuggling is captured by including the tax differential with a low cigarette tax state (North Carolina). Contrary to Baltagi and Levin (1986), they find the neighboring price variable to be statistically insignificant, whereas organized smuggling is found to be statistically significant.

There is evidence that policy makers understand that imposing tax rates above those of competing jurisdictions can negatively affect the size of their tax base. In particular, Nelson (2002) demonstrates that state legislatures are strongly influenced by the policy of adjacent states when setting tax policy on cigarettes. He also found that states with a large potential cross-border market are more likely to set rates strategically to attract nonresident customers for cigarettes and "thereby" export tax burden to non residents. A well-known case where this is presumed to occur is the state of New Hampshire, setting tax rates on tobacco (and alcohol) below that of neighboring Massachusetts to attract cross-border sales. Nelson shows that such strategic behavior extends to other states as well.

---

4 In an earlier study the ACIR (1985) deemed these 15 states in the USA to be bootlegging free: Alaska, Arizona, California, Colorado, Georgia, Hawaii, Kansas, Mississippi, Maryland, Montana, Nebraska, Nevada, New Mexico, North Dakota and South Dakota.

While the preponderance of empirical work in the USA focuses on smuggling and tax differentials among the states, Thursby and Thursby (2000) show that the Federal tax rate on cigarettes influences the level of commercial smuggling into the USA from other countries. In particular, they estimate that a 10 percent increase in the federal tax rate reduces the market share of cigarettes not smuggled by 0.8 percent.

In recognition of the real or perceived smuggling activity of all types in the 1970s, the US Government passed the Cigarette Contraband Act (CCA) in 1978. This Act made the commercial smuggling of cigarettes (shipments, sale, or purchase of more than 60,000 cigarettes not bearing the tax stamp for the state where they are found) a federal offense. The legislation also created a federal agency that was in charge of checking cigarette smuggling, the Bureau of Alcohol, Tobacco and Firearms. Interestingly, and contrary to widely-held views, Thursby and Thursby (2000) find that CCA did not deter commercial (illegal) cigarette smuggling, primarily because of a reduction in the level of enforcement activities after the law was passed.

Finally, researchers have used various techniques to account for the bias in elasticity estimates introduced by cigarette smuggling. In the quasi-experimental method discussed in Chapter 2, Baltagi and Goel (1987) control for the bootlegging effect by altering the control group to include bootlegging-free states only. The bootlegging-free states experienced only non-price influences on cigarette demand and were largely free of any biases introduced by bootlegging of cigarettes. They found that correction for bootlegging led to a lower price elasticity (that is less elastic demand) than otherwise. For instance, a 10 percent increase in the per-pack price of cigarettes from 1965 to 1971 reduced cigarette consumption by 3.7 percent when correction for bootlegging was made, as opposed to a 4.3 percent reduction when no correction was made over the same period.

International Evidence on Tobacco Smuggling

Tobacco smuggling worldwide grew by an estimated 110 percent during the decade of the nineties (*World Tobacco File*, 1998, p. 1322). By the end of the century, contraband cigarettes represented between six to nine percent of worldwide domestic cigarette sales (Joossens and Raw (1998); Merriman, Yurekli and Chaloupka (2000)). The 6 percent estimate is based on a comparison of worldwide cigarette export and import figures. Imports in 2002 were estimated to be only two-thirds of exports suggesting that the difference may have been smuggled (USDA, 2002). Since nearly 18 percent of worldwide tobacco production was exported, the export-import gap implies that smuggling accounted for a roughly 6 percent market share.[5]

Merriman, Yurekli and Chaloupka (2000) report estimates of cigarette smuggling by experts from a substantial number of developed and developing countries in 1995.[6] The population-weighted market share of smuggled cigarettes averaged 9.5 percent.

5 Of course, this is only a crude estimate subject to both upward and downward biases as discussed by Merriman, Yurekli and Chaloupka (2000), pp. 371–372.

6 Most of the data are derived from the serial, *World Tobacco File*, published by Market Tracking International.

This average masked considerable variation among individual countries; for example, the estimate for Myanmar was 53 percent, while for Nepal it was one percent.

Similar to the USA, differences in tax rates across territorial boundaries are an important determinant of the amount smuggling activity, at least in some situations. For example, between 1980 and 1994 cigarette taxes in Canada increased dramatically relative to US tax rates, standing at five times the US average at the end of the period (Sweanor and Martial, 1994). At the peak difference in rates, an estimated 30 percent of Canadian consumption represented smuggled cigarettes from the USA (Canadian Cancer Society et al., 1999), most of that derived from Canadian cigarettes exported to the USA and then illegally smuggled back into Canada (Joossens et al, 2000). The importance of smuggling in the 1980–94 period is also borne out by Galbraith and Kaiserman (1997). Making the distinction between taxed and untaxed (smuggled) cigarettes, the authors find that the tax elasticity of total cigarette sales is much lower than the tax elasticity of taxed cigarettes alone. In order to check the smuggling of cigarettes into Canada, and under heavy pressure from the tobacco industry, the Canadian Government in fact lowered cigarette taxes in 1994.[7]

Gruber et al. (2003) estimate the price elasticities of cigarette demand for Canada after controlling for the possible impacts of smuggling. This was accomplished by ignoring the years and provinces with the most severe smuggling occurrences and by using micro-level data. They find the price elasticity in a narrow range around -0.4, which incidentally is similar to the corresponding estimate for the USA (Chaloupka and Warner, 2000).

In Europe, cross-border sales (legal smuggling) are estimated to constitute about three percent of domestic consumption (Merriman, Yurekli and Chaloupka, 2000). Similar to the US, there is substantial variation in the amount of bootlegging activity among European countries, due in part to price (tax) differentials.

In contrast, legal smuggling, tax (price) differentials among countries in Europe appear to be a less important determinant of illegal (wholesale) smuggling activity. This is evident from an examination of Figure 4.1 where the price (per pack) of local brands is plotted against the estimated smuggling market share for 12 European countries. The data reveal that the contraband market share is actually lowest in some of the highest priced countries. For example, the price of a pack of cigarettes in Ireland, UK, Sweden, and Norway all exceeded US$4, yet the estimated size of the smuggled market share was less than 5 percent.[8] In contrast, Spain had the lowest cigarette price in the sample (US$1.20) yet one of the largest contraband markets.[9]

Joossens and Raw (1998) also maintain that the preponderance of wholesale smuggling activity in Europe and elsewhere is not derived from tobacco in low-price countries like Spain being smuggled into high-tax areas such as northern Europe. Instead, they argue that the international contraband market primarily consists of

---

7 In recent years Sweden also lowered cigarette taxes to make smuggling less attractive.

8 Part of the reason for low smuggling in Scandinavian countries could be that these countries have been among the least corrupt in the world (Transparency International). We test the relation between smuggling and corrupt activity in a simple model below.

9 The correlation between price and smuggling share for these observations is -0.79.

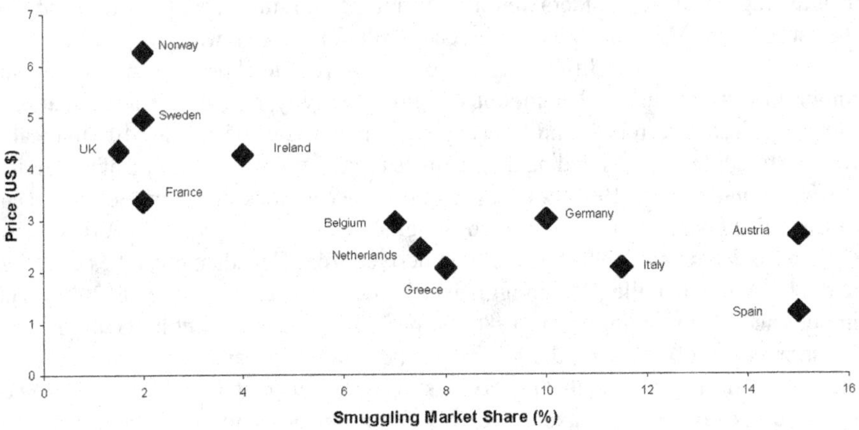

Figure 4.1 Cigarette smuggling in selected European countries (1997)
Source: Based on data from Joossens and Raw (1998)

brands produced by large multinational tobacco companies such as Marlboro and Camel, products that have a market nearly everywhere (see also Barford, 1993). The products are exported duty free from producing countries and "disappear" while in transit to the importing country. These exports never show up as official imports and hence escape the levies that would normally be imposed on such imports. A single truckload of smuggled cigarettes in such fashion is estimated to evade taxes of more than a million dollars in the European Union (Joossens and Raw, 1998, p. 150).

To examine more systematically the role of prices in international (wholesale) smuggling of cigarettes data on "expert" estimates of the smuggled market share in 1995 for 31 developed and developing countries (SMUGGLE) is regressed against relative price (RELPRICE) and per capita GDP (INCOME) variables. Here relative price is defined as the price of Marlboro cigarettes relative to the (average) price of local brands in the country under observation. RELPRICE measures the premium placed on international brands in a country with higher values representing the presence of import or other supply restrictions and/or local preferences for these brands. Accordingly, other things equal, and consistent with the predictions of the theoretical model presented above, the opportunity for smuggling is posited to be directly related to the magnitude of this price premium.[10] The resulting OLS estimate of this equation is:

$$\underset{}{\text{SMUGGLE}} = 5.53 + \underset{(1.52)}{0.84}\ \text{RELPRICE} - \underset{(2.50)}{0.0005}\ \text{INCOME} \tag{4.10}$$

10 Data sources: smuggling market share (Merriman, Yurekli and Chaloupka, 2000, Table 15.3), the price of Marlboro local brands (J. Mackay and M. Eriksen, *The Tobacco Atlas*, World Health Organization, 2002), and real GDP per capita (Summers-Heston purchasing power parity adjusted data). Nearest available data to 1995 were used in the construction of the relative price variable.

(t-statistics in parentheses) with an R-square of 0.32. The results for the price variable are consistent with hypothesis (one tail test) that the incidence of wholesale smuggling is directly related to the price premium placed on international brands of tobacco in a country. It is also clear from the above results for the income variable that smuggling market share is indirectly related to a country's level of development, a finding that is consistent with extant literature on tobacco smuggling (for example Joossens et al., 2000). Developed countries have stronger institutional arrangements and greater resources devoted to warding off such activities.[11] To formally test for the effect of the level of development, we included a dummy variable as an additional regressor in the estimated equation (4.10). This dummy variable took the value one for less-developed countries in our sample of 31 countries. The coefficient on the dummy variable was statistically insignificant and while the overall results were qualitatively similar to what is reported above, they were weaker. This suggests that the institutional differences between developed and developing nations are not easily quantifiable.

Given the data presented in Figure 4.1 and the low R-square of the above regression equation (4.10), it is clear that more factors than profit potential from selling untaxed cigarettes influence the level of smuggling activity in a country. These factors include the culture of street selling, prohibitions and restrictions on the sale of international brands, and the presence of organized crime in a country (Joossens, 1999).

There is some evidence that the tobacco industry has also played a role in worldwide tobacco smuggling. Smuggling lowers cigarette prices to consumers, directly and indirectly, and thereby increases the size of the overall market (Joossens and Raw, 1998). Prices are lowered directly through tax avoidance. Indirectly, smuggling and the loss of tax base places pressure on governments to hold down taxes, as what happened in the US in the 1970s (ACIR, 1977), or to actually lower rates, as what happened in Canada and Sweden in the nineties. Smuggling also is a way to circumvent trade barriers that make it difficult for international brands to compete.

Since the mid-nineties there have been several court cases brought against multinational tobacco companies alleging that these firms were involved in selling contraband cigarettes. For example, the European Commission (EC) made such a claim, asking for financial compensation for lost taxes and a change in policy (BBC News, 2001). The EC did not prevail in this matter but other investigations and court cases continue.[12]

Merriman, Yurekli and Chaloupka (2000) recommend coordinated multilateral policies regarding cigarette taxes to curb the smuggling of cigarettes. Given

---

11 In preliminary analysis (not reported) two variables were alternatively added to the estimating equation, a measure of the perceived level of corruption in a country (source: Transparency International) and a measure of the size of a country's black market (source: Heritage Foundation). These variables were never statistically significant and the coefficient on the income variable also became statistically insignificant, reflecting the high degree of correlation between a country's level of development and corrupt/black market activity.

12 See http://www.ash.org.uk/smuggling/ for additional listings.

multilateral action, the authors find that cigarette taxes increases would both reduce consumption and raise revenues, a finding that would be consistent with an inelastic cigarette demand. In equation (4.6) above our theoretical analysis has shown that in the absence of multilateral agreements, unilateral tax increases by a country would encourage cigarette smuggling.

Effect of the Internet

The recent proliferation of the Internet, where Internet sites hawking low-tax or no-tax tobacco products, pose additional problems for regulators trying to curb cigarette smuggling. As of 2002, there were an estimated 147 websites in the USA alone, representing 122 different vendors, selling tobacco products over the Internet (GAO 2002). Internet sales of cigarettes are growing rapidly and are expected to constitute at least one-fifth of the market by 2010 (Cohen, Sarabia and Ashley, 2001).

Nearly 60 percent of the websites in the US are located on Native American reservations where tobacco is not subject to federal and state taxes (GAO 2002). The US courts have ruled it illegal to sell tax-free cigarettes to non-Indians, but it has proved difficult to enforce this ruling. Other Internet vendors are located in low-tax states. While it is not illegal to purchase tobacco from vendors in low-tax states, consumers are legally liable to pay all state and local levies applicable in the jurisdiction in which they reside. Moreover, the Jenkins Act (15 U.S.C. 375–378) requires vendors to report the names and addresses of their customers to the home state of that buyer.

The GAO (2002) reports that none of the 147 websites it surveyed displayed information stating that they complied with the Jenkins Act and 78 percent indicated explicitly that they do not report such information to state taxing authorities. One website, for example, prominently displays on its homepage a statement that they do "not release, sell or submit to any agency or anyone else our customers' tax, personal or financial information" (http://www.indiansmokesonline.com/).

According to one research firm, states are estimated to lose up to US$200 million annually in tax revenues from such sales over the Internet. By 2005, the total revenue loss to the states could add to US$1.4bn given the growth in Internet sales (Forrester Research, 2001).

Beyond the lost tax revenues, the Internet sites also present a viable alternative for underage consumers to purchase tobacco products. Less than half of all sites require that buyers demonstrate that they are of legal ages and one in five make no mention of the fact that sales to minors are prohibited (Campaign for Tobacco-free Kids).

Some states have taken action on their own to address these problems. For example, New York made it illegal to purchase cigarettes by mail order or over the Internet. As of 2002, the US Court of Appeals has rejected legal challenges against this legislation by the tobacco companies. To deal with these issues more comprehensively, legislation proposed at the Federal level by Congressmen Martin Meehan (D – Massachusetts) and James Hansen (R – Utah) would require Internet retailers to register with the states where they sell their products and to comply with all applicable state laws. The legislation would also require Internet sellers to verify the age of their customers. The General Accounting Office has also recommended the shifting of lead enforcement of the Jenkins Act from the FBI to the Bureau of Alcohol, Tobacco, and Firearms.

Chapter Summary

In this chapter, we have focused on smuggling of tobacco products across jurisdictional boundaries. Smuggling undermines governmental efforts to generate revenues and/or curb smoking. We have presented theoretical and empirical analyses regarding the determinants of cigarette smuggling. The theoretical results of a simple model are in accord with intuition in that low taxes, high penalties, greater enforcement and low regulations all reduce smuggling.

Besides international evidence on cigarette smuggling, what is missing in the literature is study of effects of socioeconomic variables on cigarette smuggling (see Saba et al. (1995) for a notable exception). Do educational and/or religious differences across states have a significant bearing on the extent of cigarette smuggling? Are states with relatively large teenage populations experiencing more smuggling than states with a relatively large number of elderly? Do non-price factors, such as territorial restrictions on smoking, spur cigarette smuggling?[13] Our theoretical analysis above has shown that greater non-price restrictions would encourage smuggling. However, empirical evidence on this is awaited.

A number of proposals have been suggested to curb the illegal trade in cigarettes. These include: 1) Reduction in supply of cigarettes; 2) Sales restrictions; 3) Coordinated tax increases among neighboring countries; 4) Revision of penalties for smuggling; and 5) Prominent display on cigarette packages of taxes having being paid. Blanket international agreements such as the recent Framework Convention on Tobacco Control (see Chapter 9) seek to address some of these issues.

Appendix

Table A4.1 Cigarette smuggling

Country	*Price/pack (US$ 1995)*	*Smuggling (% domestic sales)*
Argentina	1.38	14
Austria	2.96	15
Azerbaijan	NA	13
Bangladesh	0.09	38
Belgium-Luxembourg	3.32	7

13 Joossens et al. (2000) is one of the rare studies that recognizes the influence of non-price factors on cigarette smuggling. However, these authors focus on corruption and organized crime as non-price factors. The impact on non-price smoking regulations on cigarette smuggling has not been considered in the literature.

Belarus	NA	23
Brazil	1.05	15
Bulgaria	0.31	15
Cambodia	0.05	37
Canada	3.98	na
China	0.1	4
Colombia	0.06	30
Czech Rep.	0.33	7
Estonia	NA	16
France	2.9	2
Germany	3.38	10
Greece	1.9	8
Hong Kong	1.58	10
Hungary	0.52	5
India	0.37	1
Indonesia	0	5
Ireland	1.69	4
Italy	2.19	12
Kazakhstan	NA	17
Latvia	NA	39
Lithuania	NA	30
Malaysia	0.68	18
Myanmar	0.56	53
Nepal	0.08	1
Netherlands	2.99	8
Pakistan	0.28	30
Philippines	0.22	19
Poland	0.37	15
Romania	0.04	20
Russia	0.03	6
Korea Rep	0.77	9
Singapore	2.24	2
Slovakia	0.38	3
Spain	1.38	15
Sri Lanka	1.05	10
Sweden	4.58	2
Taiwan	0.88	14
Thailand	0.6	11
UK	4.16	2
US	1.94	NA
Ukraine	NA	5
Uzbekistan	NA	11
Vietnam	0.1	28

Source: Jha-Chaloupka (2000), pp. 373–74.

Chapter 5

Cigarette Advertising and Bans

Introduction

Various means are used by cigarettes companies to advertise their products, including media, in-store displays, coupons, sports promotion, and so on. Now the Internet has entered the advertising arena in a significant way and limited the scope of jurisdictional controls.[1] Cigarette advertising expands the demand for cigarettes by bringing in new smokers (or inducing existing smokers to smoke more often). This is the traditional justification for advertising by cigarette firms. However, market structure considerations might force firms to advertise even when the total market is not expanding. In such cases, firms advertise to maintain or gain market share; that is, advertising is "cannibalistic". In practice, advertising might be expanding the market at the same time it reshuffles market share.[2]

Policymakers are interested in checking cigarette advertising as a non-tax measure to control smoking. Given the habit-persistence attributes of cigarettes, it is particularly important that advertising directed to youth be monitored. However, as we will show below, empirical evidence on the impact of advertising is mixed.

To put the topic discussed in this chapter in perspective, Figure 5.1 displays the trend in cigarette advertising and promotion expenditures over the 1975–2003 period for the USA. The data include advertising expenditures by tobacco companies in all settings, including magazines, newspapers, and billboards.[3] It is clear from examining this graph that tobacco companies made considerable effort to offset the negative health news and increased social stigma associated with smoking during this time period. Real advertising expenditures increased five-fold between 1975 and the early nineties, declined somewhat during the middle of the nineties, then increased again rapidly over the remainder of the time period. As of 2003, total advertising and promotional expenditures in the USA stood at US$15 billion dollars in nominal terms.

The rest of the chapter is organized as follows. First, we provide theoretical background on the role of advertising. Then we summarize the extant literature on cigarette advertising, paying special attention to the available international evidence.

---

1 These qualitative differences in the nature of advertising pose problems for empirically determining the effect of advertising. This is discussed in detail below.

2 Duffy (1996b), however, found no evidence in UK data that advertising expands the total demand for cigarettes.

3 Source: Federal Trade Commission, Cigarette Report for 2003, issued 2005, http://www.ftc.gov/reports/cigarette05/050809cigrpt.pdf. Expenditure data are deflated by the GDP deflator.

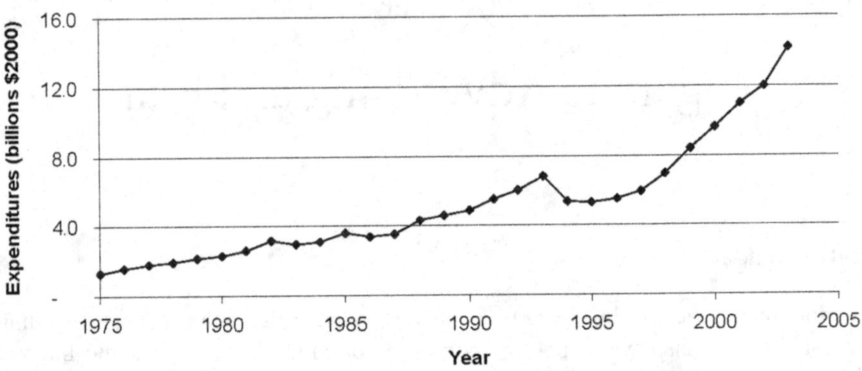

Figure 5.1 US advertising expenditures: 1975–2003

In doing so, we will also evaluate the effects of different policies related to checking cigarette advertising. Finally, we conclude this chapter by summarizing the state of the literature on this topic and suggesting directions for future research.

Advertising Elasticity

The advertising elasticity measures the responsiveness of the quantity demanded to changes in advertising and is generally a positive number (recall that advertising can sometimes be ineffective). For example, the advertising elasticity for cigarettes would tell us that for a given percent change in advertising, say 10 percent, what would be the percentage change in cigarette demand. Not only is this information useful to cigarette manufacturers, policy makers are also interested in advertising elasticity. A high advertising elasticity would invite advertising bans or restrictions as policymakers look for non-tax means of controlling smoking.

In the case of cigarettes there is some sentiment that cigarette advertising is cannibalistic in that additional advertising is just redistributing consumers among producers, rather than creating new smokers. Under these circumstances, producers would in fact welcome advertising bans as bans save wasteful spending and increase profitability. We demonstrate this below in a theoretical model that draws on the work of Tremblay and Tremblay (1999).

Given a demand function of the general form:

$$Q = f(P, A, X, R) \tag{5.1}$$

Where Q is (per capita) cigarette consumption, P is per-unit price, A is per capita advertising spending, X is a vector of other variables including income, related prices, and so on, and R is a vector of regulatory variables.

The corresponding advertising elasticity can be derived as:

$$\varepsilon_A = (\partial Q/\partial A)\,(A/Q) \tag{5.2}$$

Given an estimate of the advertising elasticity, one can determine the (percentage) change in quantity demanded for every percent change in cigarette advertising. Tremblay and Tremblay (1999) propose a more general version of (5.1) where advertising has both direct and indirect (via P) effects on cigarette demand. Formally, the demand function may now be written as

$$Q = f(P(\eta(A)), A, X, R) \tag{5.3}$$

Here η captures the degree of price competition such that a larger value of η signifies absence of price competition or the presence of market power.[4]

From (5.3), the total effect of advertising on demand in the general demand case can be shown as

$$(dQ/dA) = (\partial Q/\partial A) + (\partial Q/\partial P)\,(\partial P/\partial \eta)\,(\partial \eta/\partial A) \tag{5.4}$$

In (5.4) $(\partial Q/\partial A)$ is the direct effect of advertising on demand, and the second term captures the indirect advertising effect via price or the market structure. A negatively sloping demand signifies that $(\partial Q/\partial P)$ is negative, and an increase in market power raises the price $(\partial P/\partial \eta) > 0$. The sign of $(\partial \eta/\partial A)$ is not clear a priori as it depends on how advertising affects market power (see Leahy, 1997) for a review of the empirical literature that finds the relation between advertising and market concentration to be unclear). $(\partial \eta/\partial A)$ would be negative when greater advertising lowers market power. Such would be the case when advertising is largely of informative nature. Persuasive advertising, on the other hand, would lead to a positive $(\partial \eta/\partial A)$.

When advertising has no direct effect on cigarette demand (that is $(\partial Q/\partial A) = 0$ in (5.4)), greater informative advertising would lead to greater effect of advertising on cigarette consumption, while greater persuasive advertising would lead to lower cigarette consumption. Hence, in the absence of direct advertising effects, the market power effects of advertising can have different impacts of advertising on cigarette consumption. In fact, even with nonzero direct advertising effects (that is $(\partial Q/\partial A) > 0$), it is possible that, given the relative magnitudes of the two terms in (5.4), the overall effect of advertising could be negative in the case of persuasive advertising.

In light of these differing effects, it is understandable how a ban on cigarette advertising could have different effects. For instance, in the case of informative advertising, a ban on cigarette advertising would reduce smoking, while a similar ban on persuasive advertising would boost smoking. Cigarette manufacturers would then be in favor of a ban on persuasive advertising. This theoretical background underscores the importance of recognizing the differing nature of advertising and of paying attention to the underlying structure of cigarette markets. Research on empirical estimations of market structures is gaining importance (Hirschberg et al. 2003). These efforts are hampered in large part by the inability to get an adequate handle on the simultaneity between advertising and market structure (Leahy, 1997).

---

4 Tremblay and Tremblay (1999) note that another interpretation of η might be that it can be viewed as a price – markup term, $P = MC + \eta Q$. In competition, when $\eta = 0$, the firm uses marginal cost pricing and non-competitive markets, with $\eta > 0$, imply $P > MC$.

Estimating the Effect of Advertising

The general format for ascertaining the effect of advertising is by the inclusion of advertising as a separate regressor in a demand equation as shown in (2.1). Formally, the estimated equation might take a general form along these lines:

$$Qt = \alpha_0 + \alpha_1 Pt + \alpha_2 At + \alpha_3 Yt + \alpha_4 Xt + \alpha_5 Rt + \varepsilon_t \qquad (5.5)$$

Here Qt is the per capita cigarette consumption at time t, P is the price per pack, A is per capita advertising spending, Y is per capita disposable income, X is a vector of other shift variables (for example prices of other tobacco products) and R captures the effect of regulatory interventions. ε_t is a well-behaved error term and α_0 is a constant term. From the law of demand, the sign of α_1 is expected to be negative and that on the income coefficient (α_3) would be positive. The sign of the advertising coefficient (α_2) would be positive in the case of persuasive advertising and negative when the advertising is largely informative, dissipative or where the accompanying health warnings are more powerful than the pro-consumption advertising content. The signs of α_4 and α_5 would capture the effectiveness of respective variables in the model. Given the quality of data, one could add religious, educational and cultural variables to the right-hand-side (RHS) of (5.5). The nature of data and the sample size would also have some bearing on the choice of estimation technique (Nelson (2006) and Saffer and Chaloupka (2000) provide excellent reviews of the related literature).

Since the effect of advertising can linger over several time periods, economists have recognized that lagged advertising variables should be included in (5.5).[5] More generally, advertising can be seen as building goodwill for firms that induces consumers to buy their products (Doroodian and Seldon, 1991 and Seldon and Doroodian, 1989). Denoting the depreciation rate of goodwill by ρ, a firm's goodwill at time t (Gt) is a function of its past advertising spending:

$$Gt = At + (1\text{-}\rho)\, At_{-1} + (1\text{-}\rho)^2\, At_{-2} + \ldots \qquad (5.6)$$

Given generally finite time horizons and ineffectiveness of very distant advertising, there would be less justification for imposing an infinite lag structure on (5.6). However, in certain special cases, there might be a one time advertising spending that is expected to last infinitely into the future. Examples of such scenarios include firms paying for naming right to sports stadia, billboards at strategic places (Times Square), or sponsorship of unique events (bicentennial celebrations of independence), and so on. In this case (5.6) would become a geometric series of the form:

$$Gt = At + (1\text{-}\rho)\, At + (1\text{-}\rho)^2\, At + \ldots \quad = At/\rho \qquad (5.7)$$

5 As discussed elsewhere in Chapter 2, dynamic demand models require the addition of lagged consumption to capture the addictive influences of tobacco products.

As a practical matter, firms are likely to have advertising that fits characteristics of both (5.6) and (5.7). Empirical estimations of cigarette demand have not yet recognized this distinction, probably due to a lack of adequate data.

In general, the econometric investigations into the effect of advertising and other promotional campaigns by tobacco companies have concluded that these initiatives have had only modest positive effects on overall consumption (Jha et al., 2006). Instead, these efforts seem more effective at redistributing market share among the tobacco companies.

Effectiveness of Cigarette Advertising Bans

Bans on cigarette advertising are quite prevalent across the globe as regulators try to reduce the possibility of new consumers, especially youth, being tempted to start smoking. Boddewyn (1994) cites three primary reasons for justifying advertising bans on tobacco products: 1) restrictions on cigarette advertising will help reduce smoking to some target level; 2) tobacco manufacturers should not be allowed to undermine anti-smoking efforts by glorifying smoking in advertisements; and 3) spending on tobacco advertising substantially exceeds spending on anti-smoking advertising. Various entities all over the world are involved in banning cigarette advertising. These include governments (for example Canada, France, New Zealand, USA), international organizations (for example The World Health Organization), supranational institutions (for example The European Union), and various health associations (Boddewyn, 1994, p. 311). There exists considerable variance among tobacco advertising restrictions across countries. Roemer (1993), p. 291, reports the extent of tobacco advertising restrictions among developed nations in the seventies and eighties. On the one hand, countries like Iceland, Finland, Norway and Portugal were the early leaders in banning tobacco advertising in all media. On the other hand, some countries, such as Greece, Japan and Spain, had no tobacco advertising restrictions over the same period. Given this difference in policies, and with different socio-economic conditions across countries, international comparisons of the effectiveness of smoking restrictions will shed important light on the ability of governments to control smoking. See Table 5.2 for cross country advertising bans.

Restrictions on cigarette advertising may be viewed as part of an overall regulation of the cigarette industry. McGowan (1995) suggests that the regulation of the cigarette industry in the USA might be seen in terms of three "waves of regulation". The first wave spanned the years 1911–1964 and was primarily focused on market structure/power issues. Government in this period was concerned with checking the abuse of market power by cigarette firms. The next wave covered 1964–1985 and was concerned with the health of the smoker. This period began with the US Surgeon General's report on health risks of smoking in 1964. The current wave, starting in 1985, addresses the rights of the nonsmoker (also referred to as second-hand smoke). The last period has also involved restrictions on smoking in public places. Similar regulatory trends can also be seen in other countries (for example, Townsend (1987) cites instances of UK).

In 1971, the USA banned the advertising of cigarettes in all broadcast media. This broadcast advertising ban was preceded from 1968 to 1970 by the Fairness Doctrine that subsidized anti-smoking messages. Cigarette advertising spending in the USA surrounding the period of these policy initiatives is displayed in Figure 5.2 (Source: Eckard, 1991). It is clear from these data that the cigarette industry made up for the loss in broadcast advertising by increasing advertising in other media after the ban, most notably in-store advertising and in sports arena.

One of the earliest studies of the effect of advertising restrictions on cigarette demand is due to Schmalensee (1972). Researchers have used data at different levels of aggregation, examined different time periods and employed various estimation techniques for determining the effectiveness of policy measures in reducing cigarette consumption. A detailed review of some of the literature follows.

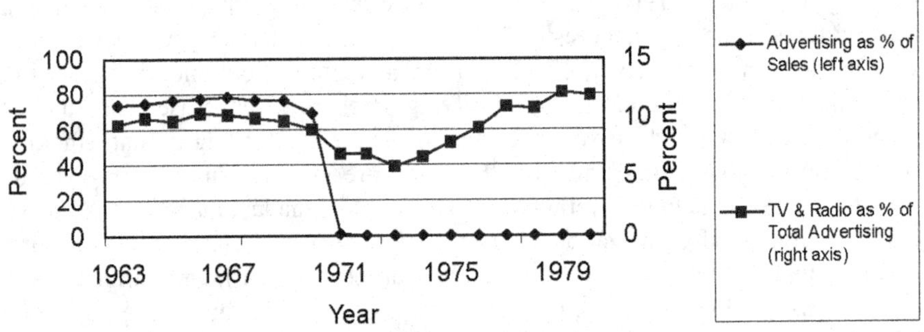

Figure 5.2 US cigarette industry advertising

a. Effects on all consumers

Numerous studies use state-level US data pooled over time to study cigarette demand. These studies are summarized in the top panel of Table 5.1. Part of the reason for the proliferation of studies at this level of aggregation is the easy availability of most of these data from The Tobacco Institute. Using state-level US data, Baltagi and Levin (1986) found mild support for the effectiveness of the subsidized anti-smoking messages under the Fairness Doctrine in curbing cigarette consumption. Using annual state-level US data for 1952–82, Goel and Morey (1995) focused on the simultaneity between cigarette and liquor consumption (that is the cross-price elasticities between cigarettes and liquor). Contrary to most of the literature, they found the broadcast advertising ban to be effective in reducing cigarette consumption.[6] Similar to Goel and Morey's (1995) findings with aggregate state-level pooled data, Keeler et al. (1993) also found smoking restrictions in California to be effective in reducing smoking. In another panel data study, Keeler et al. (1996) use state-level data for US spanning the period 1960–90. The new "twist" in this

6 Both Baltagi and Levin (1986) and Goel and Morey (1995) use dummy variables to capture the effect of the advertising ban.

study is that it examines whether cigarette firms price-discriminate across states by looking at the effects on the retail price of cigarettes. The authors find that cigarette firms do price discriminate across states and that the regulatory anti-smoking efforts are countered by cigarette producers by lowering cigarette prices. There is some evidence regarding the ineffectiveness of restrictions on smokeless tobacco as well (Goel and Nelson, 2005).

Advertising restrictions on cigarettes are prevalent in other countries besides the USA. In fact, restrictions on smoking in some countries are more stringent than those in the USA. Australia has quite extensive curbs on cigarette advertising, including restriction on advertising in the electronic media. Using Australian data, Bardsley and Olekalns (1999) found that whereas workplace smoking bans and health warnings were effective in reducing smoking, anti-smoking advertisements and bans on electronic media advertising were ineffective. An earlier study by Clements et al. (1985) found a significant impact of advertising on cigarette demand in UK and Australia. The effects of smoking regulations and cigarette taxation in Canada were examined by Lanoie and Leclair (1998). Two alternate forms of the dependent variables were used in this study, namely, cigarette consumption and the percentage of smokers in the population. Smoking regulations were found to be ineffective. The interesting result in this study is that these findings are reversed when the dependent variable is the proportion of smokers, and not total cigarette consumption. Townsend (1987) used data on individuals in UK and found the ban on electronic media advertising to be ineffective in reducing smoking. When pooled samples of OECD countries are studied to determine the effectiveness of advertising bans in controlling cigarette consumption, it appears that the evidence is mixed. While some studies have found such bans to be effective in reducing smoking (Laugesen and Meads, 1991), others have found that these bans in fact lead to higher cigarette consumption (Stewart, 1993). See Table 5.1.

While some of the data might be dated, Roemer (1993), p. 291, provides excellent international comparisons of the effectiveness of tobacco advertising bans. Countries were placed in four groups based on the extent of tobacco advertising restrictions: i) countries enforcing complete tobacco advertising bans (Iceland, Finland, Norway, Portugal); ii) countries allowing tobacco advertising in few media (Belgium, France, Italy, New Zealand, Singapore, Sweden); iii) countries allowing tobacco advertising in most media (Australia, Austria, Belgium, Canada, Denmark, France, the Federal Republic of Germany, Ireland, Netherlands, Switzerland, UK, USA);[7] and iv) countries allowing tobacco promotion in all media (Greece, Japan and Spain). Total advertising bans (group (i)) were most successful in reducing smoking. Interestingly, Roemer finds no difference in the smoking reducing efficacy of policies that allow advertising in most media and cases where there are no restrictions on tobacco advertising (that is between groups (iii) and (iv)). The World Health Organization (1996) reports that in the early 1990s, 27 countries had total or almost total bans on cigarette advertising. This number had, however, decreased to 18 by mid-1990s.

---

7 Countries appearing in more than one group are those where there are multiple studies covering different smoking bans. Some countries might have further changed their policies since these studies were conducted.

A large part of the ambiguity regarding the effect of advertising restriction policies on cigarette demand appears to be due to the fact that the underlying relation between advertising and cigarette demand has not been well understood. Most studies model advertising restrictions as a 1–0 dichotomous variable that takes on a value of one for the period after the policy is implemented (or vice versa). Some studies have found the effects of contemporaneous advertising on smoking to be negative (Baltagi and Levin, 1992; Goel and Morey, 1995) and a positive effect with a lag (Goel and Morey, 1995). Doorodian and Seldon (1991) use an extensive lag structure on advertising to determine its effects on US cigarette demand. They found the short-run advertising elasticity of 0.6 and the corresponding long-term elasticity of 0.20. In light of this, perhaps a lag structure on the effects of regulation is also called for.

There are a few studies that focus on regional cigarette demand, most notably California. In an interesting study that examines regulation at the state-level, Hu, Sung and Keeler (1995b) examine the effects of the California Tobacco Tax and Health Promotion Act. This Act not only raised cigarette taxes but also earmarked some of the tax revenues for health education programs to reduce cigarette consumption. While the authors found both positive and negative cigarette advertisements to be effective, advertising was not the most cost-effective way to alter consumer preferences.

b. Effects on teen smoking

It is important to separately study the effects of cigarette advertising on teenagers because young people might respond differently to advertising messages. Further, very few people begin smoking after their teenage years so this is an especially important group in any long-run strategy to control tobacco consumption.[8] The success of teenage anti-smoking policies to date has been called in question by the international trend in the decline in smoking initiation age.[9] In particular, a WHO (1996) report estimates that in many countries in the early 1990s the median smoking initiation age was under 15 years.

As far as we have been able to determine, only one study has addressed the effectiveness of advertising bans and anti-smoking messages on teenage tobacco use. Pechmann and Ratneshwar (1994) exposed about 300 California 12–13 year olds who were nonsmokers to magazine advertising to determine their perceptions about peers who smoked. Subjects who saw anti-smoking advertisements judged the smoker to be relatively immature and unglamorous. In light of this, special advertising

8 Evidence of this is found in studies of all consumers where the habit-persistence effect, measured by including lagged cigarette consumption as an additional regressor in the estimated equation of cigarette demand, is found to be significant (for example, Baltagi and Levin, 1986 and Goel and Morey, 1995).

9 Examples of policies targeted specifically to teenage smoking include restrictions on sale of tobacco products to teenagers, restrictions on advertising in the vicinity of schools, and so on. In the early 1990s about 25 countries had regulations prohibiting the sale of cigarettes to minors (WHO, 1996).

campaigns are being targeted to prevent teen smoking. Such advertisements stress situations related to smoking that teens perceive as "uncool". There is an obvious need for more research on the responses of teenagers to cigarette advertising.

c. Conclusions regarding the effectiveness of cigarette advertising restrictions

The overall impact of advertising restrictions on cigarette consumption varies across studies, driven primarily by the nature of data and the estimation techniques (see Table 5.1). Some studies have used aggregated data sets, while others have been able to use data at lower levels of aggregation. The time periods covered in the analyses of cigarette demand have varied, although almost all studies focus on the latter half of the twentieth century. In the case of the USA, most studies have focused on the effect of the broadcast advertising ban imposed in 1971. This measure banned all cigarette advertising on radio and television. The evidence in the literature regarding the effectiveness of this ban seems to be mixed.[10]

Nelson (2006) provides a useful meta-analysis of the research on cigarette advertising regulation in the USA over the past 50 years. This period included four significant events: 1) the 1953 health scare; 2) the 1964 Surgeon General's Report regarding the ill-health effects of smoking; 3) the 1968–1970 Fairness Doctrine; and 4) the 1971 ban on broadcast advertising of cigarettes. The review shows the effect of broadcast ban to be insignificant. It would be interesting to see how governments are able to regulate advertising messages in digital media that span across jurisdictional boundaries (for example the Internet).

10 Duffy (1996a, p.19) concludes in his survey of the literature on advertising restrictions: "There are results pointing in both directions in these studies with respect to the impact upon demand of advertising bans. On the basis of this review, however, we are left with the definite impression that the weight of the evidence in these studies does not give much support, if any, to those who believe that advertising bans are an effective means of reducing consumption."

Table 5.1 Effectiveness of cigarette advertising restrictions

Study	*Data*	*Effectiveness of advertising restrictions in reducing smoking*
	US studies: Using aggregate data	
Baltagi and Levin (1986)	US, annual state-level,1963–80	Broadcast ban ineffective
Doroodian and Seldon (1991)	US, annual aggregate,1952–84	Restrictions effective
Goel and Morey (1995)	US, annual state-level, 1959–82	Broadcast ban effective
Goel and Nelson (2005)	US, annual state-level, 1997	Advertising restrictions ineffective across gender and age, and across cigarettes and smokeless tobacco (*)
Hu et al. (1995b)	California, monthly,1980–93	Both tax and media restrictions had negative impact on consumption
Seldon and Doroodian (1989)	US, annual aggregate,1952–84	Media policy coefficients negative but statistically insignificant
Sung et al. (1994)	US, annual state-level,1967–90	Broadcast ban ineffective
	US studies: Using micro data	
Czart et al. (2001)	US, college students,1997	Cigarette billboard advertising bans effective; student newspaper bans ineffective
	International studies: Using aggregate data	
Cameron (1997)	Greece	Effect of TV advertising ban insignificant
Cox and Smith (1984)	15 OECD countries, annual, 1962–80	Legislative restrictions more effective than voluntary restrictions
Johnson (1986)	Australia, annual,1961–62 to 1982–83	Effect of electronic media advertising ban insignificant
Lanoie and Leclair (1998)	Canada, provincial,1980–95	Effects of anti-smoking regulation mixed (*)
Laugesen and Meads (1991)	22 OECD countries, annual, 1960–86	Advertising restrictions effective in reducing smoking
Roemer (1993)	24 countries, 1970–86	Comprehensive advertising bans most effective in reducing smoking
Saffer and Chaloupka (2000)	22 OECD countries, annual, 1970–92	Comprehensive bans effective in reducing smoking; partial bans have little or no effect
Stewart (1993)	22 OECD countries, annual, 1964–90	Advertising bans led to a small, statistically insignificant, increase in average smoking
	International studies: Using micro data	
Townsend (1987)	UK, annual, adults, 1961–77	Electronic media ban ineffective in reducing consumption

Note: (*) denotes that the study uses an index of regulation. See Goel and Nelson (2006).

Chapter Summary

From the extant literature on the advertising regulations on tobacco, the effectiveness of such regulation is still not clear. In sum, while our understanding of the behavior of smokers and their responses to advertising has improved in recent times, there is a need for more research using micro-level data including more research focusing on population subgroups such as teenagers, religious and ethnic groups. There also appears to be a need for better modeling of effects of regulation besides using standard dummy variables. A cross-country survey including consistent data for various countries would facilitate international comparisons.

The recent advances in telecommunications have opened up new avenues for advertisers. The most notable development in this regard is the explosive growth of the Internet. Now smokers in a particular jurisdiction are susceptible to advertising from other (unregulated) jurisdictions. This would further undermine the ability of authorities to institute effective policy measures.

Table 5.2 Growth in cigarette consumption (per capita adults 15–64) 1981–91 and media bans

1 = comprehensive adv bans
2 = no comp ban
3 = former communist

					Smoking prevalence various years (% adult >15)	
Country	*growth cig cons*	*ban*	*high inc*	*OECD*	*men*	*women*
Afghanistan	-0.125	1				
Albania	-0.008	2			50	8
Algeria	0.013	1			53	10
Argentina	-0.09	2			40	23
Australia	-0.212	2	1	1	27	23
Austria	-0.156	2	1	1	39	24
Bahamas			1		19	4
Bahrain					24	6
Bangladesh	0.456	2			60	15
Belgium	-0.198	2	1	1	31	19
Benin	-0.156	2				
Bolivia	-0.232	2			50	21
Brazil	-0.143	2			40	25
Bulgaria	0.191	3			38	17
Cambodia	-0.032	2				
Cameroon	0.254	2				
Canada	-0.332	1	1	1	31	29
Chile	-0.181	2			38	25
China	0.473	3			63	4
Colombia	-0.022	2			35	19
Congo	0.011	2				
Cook Island					44	26

Costa Rica	-0.118	2			35	20
Cote D Ivorie	-0.123	2				
Cuba	-0.133	3			49	25
Cyprus			1		43	7
Czech Rep.					43	13
Denmark	-0.054	2	1	1	54	46
Dominican Rep	0	2			66	14
Ecuador	0.048	2				
Egypt	0.025	2			40	1
El Salvador	-0.019	2			38	12
Estonia					54	24
Ethiopia	0.286	2				
Fiji					59	31
Finland	-0.033	1	1	1	27	19
France	0.019	2	1	1	40	27
Germany	-0.025	2	1	1	31	18
Ghana	-0.432	2				
Greece	0.044	2	1	1	46	28
Guatemala	-0.469	2			38	18
Honduras	-0.213	2			36	11
Hungary	-0.018	3			40	27
Iceland	-0.115	1	1	1	31	28
India	0.046	2			40	3
Indonesia	0.242	2			53	4
Iran	-0.198	2				
Iraq	0.174	1			40	5
Ireland	-0.201	2	1	1	30	28
Israel	-0.046	2	1		45	30
Italy	-0.169	1	1	1	34	17
Jamaica	-0.131	2			43	13
Japan	-0.055	2	1	1	59	15
Jordan	-0.087	1				
Kenya	-0.107	2				
Korea Rep	0.095	2	1	1	68	7
Kuwait			1		52	12
Laos P.D.R.	0	2				
Latvia					56	11
Lesotho					38	1
Lithuania					53	8
Luxembourg			1	1	32	26
Madagascar	-0.021	2				
Malawi	0	2				
Malaysia	-0.205	2			41	4
Malta					40	18
Mauritius	-0.057	2			47	4
Mexico	-0.292	2			38	14

Mongolia					40	7
Morocco	-0.179	2			40	9
Mozambique	0	2				
Myanmar	0.071	2				
Nepal	1	2				
Netherlands	-0.143	2	1	1	36	29
New Zealand	-0.131	1	1	1	24	22
Nicaragua	0.014	2				
Niger	0.7	2				
Nigeria	0.057	2			24	7
Norway	-0.062	1	1	1	36	36
Pakistan	-0.111	2			36	9
Panama	0.011	2				
Papua New Guinea					46	28
Paraguay	0.068	2			24	6
Peru	-0.103	2			41	13
Philippines	-0.196	2			43	8
Poland	0.065	3			51	29
Portugal	0.117	1	1	1	38	15
Romania	-0.272	3				
Russian Fed					63	30
Samoa					53	19
Saudi Arabia	0.098	2			53	1
Senegal	0.382	2				
Seychelles					51	10
Sierra Leone	0	2				
Singapore	-0.369	1	1		32	3
Slovakia					43	26
Slovenia					35	23
South Africa	0.075	2			50	19
Spain	0.094	2	1	1	48	25
Sri Lanka	-0.173	2			55	1
Sudan	0	1			12	1
Sweden	-0.158	2	1	1	22	24
Switzerland	-0.049	2	1	1	36	26
Tanzania	0	2				
Thailand	-0.028	1			45	3
Togo	0.021	2				
Tonga					65	14
Trinidad	-0.092	2				
Tunisia	0.101	2				
Turkey	-0.067	2			63	24
Turkmenistan					27	1
Uganda	0	2				
UK	-0.193	2	1	1	29	28
Uruguay	-0.012	2			41	27

USA	-0.25	2	1	1	28	23
Uzbekistan					40	1
Venezuela	-0.131	2				
Vietnam	0	2			73	4
Yemen Rep	0.421	2				
Yugoslavia	-0.076	3				
Zambia	0	2				
Zimbabwe	-0.348	2				

Source: Jha and Chaloupka (2000) pp. 231–32; 470–76.

Chapter 6

Health Warnings

Introduction

Concerns about the ill health effects of cigarettes have prompted lawmakers to warn consumers about the health consequences of consuming tobacco products in general and cigarettes in particular. Over the last half century or so, these concerns have arisen mainly from the link between smoking and cancer. More recently, however, the focus has shifted to non-smokers as the health consequences of second-hand smoke have come to light. Further, over time the breadth of health warnings have gone beyond cigarettes to cover other tobacco products. For instance, warning labels on packages of chewing tobacco warn of the possibility of the cancer of the mouth.

Health warnings related to smoking include mandated warning labels on cigarette packages, warnings accompanying advertisements and distribution of other health materials. One could envision warning labels on cigarette packages and those accompanying advertisements as tempering the consumption-inducing effects of advertising. The size and position of the warning label on the package may also matter in this regard and this has been regulated by some countries. For example, under a recent WHO protocol, most nations of the world have agreed to mandate that at least one-third of the space of cigarette packages be devoted to anti-smoking messages, for example the recent Framework Convention on Tobacco Control (FCTC).

In this chapter we summarize current policies regarding health warnings on tobacco products and advertisements, both for the USA and internationally. We follow this up with a review of the literature on the effectiveness of such policies in reducing the consumption of tobacco products.

Health Warning Policies

In this section we outline significant tobacco health warning initiatives in various regions of the world, starting with the USA.

USA

In 1964, the US Surgeon General issued a report warning about the ill health effects of smoking. This was followed by the passage of the Federal Cigarette Labeling and Advertising Act in 1965 (Public Law 89–92). This act mandated that the warning, "Caution: Cigarette Smoking May Be Hazardous to Your Health" be displayed on the side of each cigarette pack.

This policy was followed by the Fairness Doctrine from 1968 to 1970 that subsidized anti-smoking messages. Baltagi and Levin (1992), p. 330, report that: "The value of these (Fairness Doctrine) anti-smoking messages were estimated at US$75 million in 1970. This is roughly one-third the industry's advertising expenditure on TV and radio for that year."

In 1969, Congress passed legislation (Public Law 91–222) that would replace the Fairness Doctrine by placing a ban on all cigarette advertising on television and radio. The legislation also strengthened the text of the warning labels on cigarette packages to read that, "Cigarette Smoking Is Dangerous to Your Health." In an effort to further educate the public about the health consequences of smoking, Congress passed Public Law 98–474 in 1984. This legislation required a set of four specific warnings on the adverse health consequences of smoking to be placed on all cigarette packages and advertisements in the USA on a rotating basis (for details, see Viscusi, 1993, p. 262).[1]

Recognizing the link between smokeless tobacco and health problems Congress passed legislation in 1986 (Public Law 99–252) requiring three rotating health messages on these products. That was followed in 2000 with an agreement between the FTC and the seven largest US cigar companies to place rotating warning messages on cigar products and advertisements for these products.

International

Table 6.1 summarizes the policies regarding tobacco health warnings from an international perspective. Data for individual countries can be found in the appendix. According to UICC GLOBALink, 138 countries require some type of health warnings on tobacco products as of 2003. This figure is up substantially from the early 1990s when the World Health Organization (1996) reported that only about 80 countries mandated such warnings. Most of the package health warnings/messages were the product of legislation imposed in the seventies and eighties. However, some countries such as Italy imposed mandates that predate US regulations in this area.[2]

Of the 54 countries that currently do not regulate health warnings on tobacco packages, most are either low or lower-middle income countries according to The World Bank classification system. Nearly one-half of the countries (25) that do not mandate warnings are located in Sub-Saharan Africa and another 10 are Latin American or Caribbean countries. All major Western countries have required warnings on tobacco packages. For example, a directive of the European Union in 1992 mandates all members to carry warning labels on the front and back of cigarette packages.

1 Much of the information in this section is derived from the Warning Label Fact Sheet of the US Public Health Service.

2 Italy mandated cigarette health warnings in 1962, three years before similar legislation was passed in the U.S. and Great Britain.

Table 6.1 International regulations on tobacco health warnings

Package health warning/message	*Number of countries*
Required	138
Not regulated	54
Health warnings on tobacco advertising	
Required	68
Not regulated	47
Not applicable	31
Unknown	40

Source: UICC GLOBALink – http://www.globalink.org/tccp/, 2003.
Data refer to regulations by the central government only.

Warning labels vary considerably internationally with respect to such factors as the content of the message and the size and placement on the package. There is no requirement, for example, that the US cigarette manufacturers must follow US labeling regulations for products they export to other countries. As a result, these companies typically only do what is required by the laws of the local country (Aftab et al., 1998). Some countries have stronger laws than what is required in the USA; for instance, Canada warnings on cigarette packages sold in Canada are more prominent than those in the USA (Mahood, 1995; Health Canada, 2003). Chapman and Carter (2003) report that the "gold standard" for health warnings are graphic color photographs that were adopted in Canada (2000) and Brazil (2002). They further report that similar warning labels are planned for Malaysia, Singapore, and Australia.

In 1998, the Public Citizen's Health Research Group evaluated health warning requirements of 45 countries (27 developing and 18 developed) on a 10-point scale with respect to message content and language, its size and placement on the package, and other factors. They report an average "quality" score for all countries in their sample of 3.0 (10 = highest). The quality of the message tended to be higher in developed countries where the average score was 5.0 in comparison with developing countries with an average score of only 1.6. These averages, however, mask considerable variation among countries. For example, South Africa and Thailand received scores of 10 and 9, respectively, while the score for Japan was zero. The index for the USA was 6.0.

In the bottom half of Table 6.1, international regulations regarding health warnings on the advertising of tobacco products are summarized. Sixty-eight countries require that advertisements of tobacco products carry health warnings, 47 other countries currently do not have such mandates. In 40 countries it could not be determined if such warnings were required and in 31 countries such a requirement was presumed to be "not applicable" presumably because most forms of advertising were not permitted.

Generally, countries that did not mandate package health/warning labels also did not regulate the advertising of tobacco products. Several countries that mandate package warnings, however, do not extend this regulation to the advertisement of other tobacco products. Examples of the latter include Australia, Canada, Switzerland, and the UK.

Evidence Regarding Effectiveness of Health Warnings

We begin by reviewing and assessing the extant literature on the effectiveness of health warning on tobacco consumption in the USA. These studies are summarized in Table 6.2. Several studies focused on the efficacy of the Fairness Doctrine in reducing smoking. This doctrine required television and radio stations broadcasting cigarette commercials to donate time for anti-smoking commercials. The doctrine ended in 1971 when broadcast cigarette advertising was banned.

The evidence regarding the impact this doctrine had on reducing cigarette consumption is mixed (Nelson, 2006). Lewit, Coate and Grossman (1981) studied trends in smoking by youth during the years 1966–1970, a period before and during the Fairness Doctrine. The authors concluded that the Fairness Doctrine "had a substantial negative impact on teenage smoking participation rates" (p. 569). More recently, Baltagi and Levin (1986) found mild support for the effectiveness of Fairness Doctrine in reducing smoking at the pooled state-level US data. The authors later examined time series of individual states and found the effect of the Fairness Doctrine to be mixed across states (Baltagi and Levin, 1992). Goel and Morey (1995), on the other hand, found that cigarette consumption *increased* due to the Fairness Doctrine. With the exception of Lewit et al., all of the aforementioned studies include observations that extend beyond the end of the Fairness Doctrine. The mixed findings of these papers may be related to problems with quantifying the effects of policy interventions via dichotomous variables that fail to capture relevant institutional details affecting tobacco consumption. Moreover, it may be problematic to disentangle empirically the somewhat overlapping effects of the broadcast ban on tobacco products and the end of subsidized anti-smoking messages, especially around 1971.

Regarding the consumption effects of health warning messages on cigarette packages, one of the earliest studies to address this was by Hamilton (1972). He found health warnings to be effective in reducing US cigarette consumption. More recently, Bishop and Yoo (1985) concluded that such warnings (for example the 1964 Surgeon General's Report linking smoking to cancer) had little effect on smoking. In contrast, Seldon and Doroodian (1989) found evidence supporting the effectiveness of health warnings in reducing cigarette consumption. All these studies used time-period dummy variables to account for the effect of packaging regulations. An interesting study by Gallet and Agarwal (1999) uses a switching regression model, instead of dummy variables, to determine the effects of health warnings on smoking in the USA. The authors find that the health warnings were gradually effective in checking cigarette consumption.

Table 6.2 Effectiveness of health warnings: US-based studies

Study	Data	Effectiveness in reducing smoking
Panel A: Studies using aggregate US data		
Baltagi and Levin (1986)	Annual state-level data, 1963–80	Fairness Doctrine effective in reducing smoking
Baltagi and Levin (1992)	Annual state-level data, 1963–88	Effects of Fairness Doctrine mixed
Bishop and Yoo (1985)	US annual aggregate data, 1954–80	Health warnings had little impact on cigarette demand
Blaine and Reed (1994)	US annual aggregate data, 1946–92	Health warnings significant in reducing smoking
Gallet and Agarwal (1999)	US annual aggregate data, 1955–90	Health warnings gradually reduce smoking
Goel and Morey (1995)	Annual state-level data, 1959–82	Fairness Doctrine increased smoking
Hamilton (1972)	US annual aggregate data, 1925–70	Health warnings effective in reducing smoking
Seldon and Doroodian (1989)	US annual aggregate data, 1952–84	Firms increase advertising in response to health warnings
Panel B: US studies using micro data		
Lewit, Coate and Grossman (1981)	US, youth, 1966–70	Fairness Doctrine effective in reducing smoking participation rates

Note: (*) denotes that the study uses an index of regulation. See also Goel and Nelson (2006).

In contrast to the literature based on US data, the preponderance of international-based studies have concluded that health warnings are an effective way to curb tobacco consumption. These studies are summarized in Table 6.3. The evidence is generally consistent for analyses based on either aggregate or micro data. Interestingly, recent studies assessing the impact of large and graphic warning labels (beyond what is currently required in the USA) have concluded that these strategies are effective in reducing tobacco consumption (see Panel B in Table 6.3). For example, after the launch of color, picture-based warnings (for example diseased mouth, lung tumors) on the front and back half of cigarette packages, a survey of Canadian smokers commissioned by the Canadian Cancer Society (2002) reported that 44 percent of smokers responded that the new warnings increased their motivation to quit smoking. Nearly a quarter responded they smoked less because of the new warnings.

Table 6.3 Effectiveness of health warnings: International-based studies

Study	Data	Effectiveness in reducing smoking
	Panel A: Studies using aggregate data	
Atkinson and Skeggs (1973)	UK, annual, 1951–70	Health warnings only temporarily effective in reducing smoking
Cameron (1997)	Greece	Anti-smoking campaign effective
Conniffe (1995)	Ireland, annual, 1960–1990	Proportion of smokers negatively affected by health warnings; smoking unaffected by health warnings
Leu (1984)	Switzerland, annual, 1954–81	Anti-smoking publicity effective in deterring cigarette consumption
Pekurinen (1989)	Finland, annual, 1960–81	Effects of anti-smoking advertising ambiguous
Radfar (1985)	UK, quarterly, 1965–80	Health warnings effective in reducing smoking
Stavrinos (1987)	Greece, annual, 1960–82	Health warnings effective in reducing smoking.
Tansel (1993)	Turkey, annual, 1960–88	Health warnings and anti-smoking campaigns effective in reducing smoking
Wilcox, Tharp and Yang (1994)	S. Korea, monthly, 1988–92	Health warnings not significant in reducing smoking; however, consumption of foreign cigarettes reduced.
Witt and Pass (1981)	UK, annual, 1955–75	Health warnings effective in reducing smoking
	Panel B studies using micro data	
Borland (1997)	*Australian* smokers, 1995	More prominent labels caused a larger percentage of smokers to refrain from smoking on at least one occasion.
Borland and Hill (1997)	*Australian* smokers, 1995	More prominent labels made smokers better informed about health risks of smoking.
Canadian Cancer Society (2002)	Canadian adults, 2001	Graphic warning labels are effective in discouraging smoking
Hammond et al. (2003)	Canadian smokers, 2001	Graphic warning labels are an effective smoking cessation intervention.
Lewit et al. (1997)	US, Canada, school students, 1990, 1992	Anti-tobacco advertising correlated with greater likelihood of smoking.
Townsend, Roderick and Cooper (1994)	UK, household data, 1972–90	Effects of health publicity significant and vary across gender
Zanias (1987)	Greece, 1974 household survey (also uses time series data)	Anti-smoking campaign significantly reduced smoking.

Note: Also see Goel and Nelson (2006).

Additional Evidence on the Relative Effectiveness of Health Warnings

New evidence on the relative effectiveness of advertising and territorial restrictions on smoking prevalence in the US states in 1997 is presented in Table 6.4. Here state advertising restrictions are measured with a zero – one dummy variable, with a value of one indicating that a state imposes additional restrictions on tobacco advertising beyond what is mandated by federal law. Examples of such restrictions include restricting billboard cigarette advertisements near schools and inside government buildings, prohibiting cigarette advertising on state run lottery tickets, and so on.[3] In the year 1997, only 13 states imposed additional advertising restrictions. Territorial restrictions are measured by the number of smoke free indoor air quality restrictions a state imposes in five different sites.[4] The range of values for this variable goes from zero (no restrictions) to five.

The results, reported as Model 1 in Table 6.4, indicate that the territorial restrictions are more effective at reducing smoking prevalence than advertising restrictions that go beyond Federal requirements. Additional restrictions on tobacco advertising appears to have no effect on smoking prevalence as the coefficient on this variable is not statistically different from zero using conventional standards of significance. In contrast, the coefficient on the territorial variable is negative – more smoke free indoor sites are associated with lower smoking prevalence – and statistically significant at better than the 5 percent level. The behavioral effect of such restrictions are modest, however, as the coefficient indicates that the imposition of one additional territorial restriction lowers the incidence of smoking by six-tenths of 1 percent.

In Model 2 the price of a pack of cigarettes (measured in cents) is added as an additional right-hand side variable.[5] The results confirm the expected negative effect that price and tax policy has on smoking prevalence. Advertising restrictions beyond Federal mandates are still ineffective at reducing the incidence of smoking. The value of coefficient on the territorial variable is reduced by one-third, but remains significant at the five-percent level (one-tail test).

3 Source: Centers for Disease Control and Prevention (CDC), *State Tobacco Control Highlights*, 1999.

4 The five sites are: government worksites, private worksites, restaurants, day care centers, and home-based day care. Source: CDC (1999).

5 Source: *The Tax Burden on Tobacco.*

Table 6.4 The effectiveness of advertising and territorial restrictions on smoking prevalence: US states, 1997

(Dependent variable: percent smokers)	Model 1	Model 2
Constant	24.84*** (29.63)	30.67*** (10.84)
Advertising restrictions	0.765 (0.84)	0.641 (0.72)
Territorial restrictions	– 0.639** (2.37)	–0.425 (1.53)
Price	–	– 0.034** (2.15)
R-square	0.12	0.20
N	51	51
F-statistic	3.31**	3.91**

Notes: Absolute value of t-statistic is in parentheses.
***denotes significance at the 1% level and **denotes significance at the 5% level.

Effect of the Internet

The spread of the Internet has opened up new possibilities both in dissemination of health warnings and in opening up avenues to by-pass existing mandates. On the one hand, government agencies can disseminate health related information quickly and cheaply with the Internet. Smokers and potential smokers in remote areas can be made aware of new research and cessation breakthroughs rapidly. On the other hand, the inability to police the Internet effectively, especially across international borders, has opened up avenues for tobacco sales/advertising from less-regulated or unregulated jurisdictions.

The use of Internet for health warnings also poses equity issues. Low-income populations do not have access to high-technology and are likely to be deprived of any benefits from such technologies. These inequities are likely to exist both in intra-national and international contexts.

Chapter Summary

The health warnings regarding tobacco consumption are still evolving. Consequently, it is difficult to gauge their impact. On the one hand, medical research is still producing new evidence linking tobacco consumption to new effects (for example, recent evidence shows that low-tar cigarettes are not as "harmless" as previously thought).[6] On the other hand, policymakers are constantly trying to devise warning labels that are effective in reaching diverse audiences across nations with variations in socio-economic aspects including differences in religious beliefs, education, gender, economic status, and age (Kenkel and Chen, 2000). How can existing cigarette

6 http://news.bbc.co.uk/1/hi/health/3379017.stm.

warning labels be modified to appeal to youth? Another complexity to all this seems to be added as the world is becoming one big global market via the Internet. In spite of all this, this chapter reviews the existing evidence on the effectiveness of tobacco health warnings and provides some new evidence of its own.

Quantitative comparisons of the effects of health warnings across different studies are problematic because some studies use dummy variables to take account of regulatory phases (for example Hamilton, 1972; Baltagi and Levin, 1986, 1992, Goel and Morey, 1995), while others use some indexes of regulation (for example Laugesen and Meads, 1991; Lanoie and Leclair, 1998, Yurekli and Zhang, 2000). One could argue that indexes of regulation are better than dummy variables in that they are broader, yet they fail to capture institutional details that are critical in cross-country comparisons. Most of the studies of tobacco consumption, use tobacco price and income as control variables, while some also include other regulations such as tobacco advertising bans (see Goel and Nelson, 2006). What we find is that control strategies should be considered simultaneously – it is the collective whole that is most effective and leaving out some aspects could lead to an omitted variable bias.

In sum, the overall evidence on the effectiveness of cigarette health warnings is mixed. These warnings have come in many forms, with the most prominent being the mandatory labels on cigarette packages. In the case of USA, the main focus has been on the effect of the Fairness Doctrine and its impact has been mixed. Some studies have found that the Fairness Doctrine in fact increased smoking (Goel and Morey, 1995). This ambiguity was probably the main impetus behind the short life of this doctrine. The main problem in ascertaining the impact of health warnings on cigarette consumption appears to be the difficulty in getting a handle on the qualitative differences among various health warnings and the related institutional details. How is the nature of certain health warnings different from others and how can this difference be adequately measured?

Appendix 1 International regulations on tobacco health warnings, 2003

Countries	*Advt. health warnings*	*Package health warnings/ messages*	*Income group*
		Region: East Asia and the Pacific	
Australia		X	High income: OECD
Brunei	uk	X	High income: nonOECD
Cambodia	x	X	Low income
China	x	X	Lower middle income
Fiji		X	Lower middle income
Indonesia	x	X	Low income
Japan	x	X	High income: OECD
Kiribati	uk		Lower middle income
Korea, Republic of	x	X	High income: OECD
Laos People's Dem. Rep.	uk	X	Low income
Malaysia	x	X	Upper middle income
Marshall Islands	uk		Lower middle income
Micronesia			Lower middle income
Mongolia		X	Low income
Myanmar	uk	X	Low income
New Zealand		X	High income: OECD
Palau			Upper middle income
Papua New Guinea	x	X	Low income
Philippines	x	X	Lower middle income
Samoa	uk	X	Lower middle income
Singapore	na	X	High income: nonOECD
Solomon Islands	na	X	Low income
Thailand		X	Lower middle income
Tonga	na	X	Lower middle income
Vanuatu	na	X	Lower middle income
Vietnam	na		Low income
		Region: Europe and Central Asia	
Albania	x		Lower middle income
Armenia	x	X	Low income
Azerbaijan	x	X	Low income
Belarus		X	Lower middle income
Bosnia and Herzegovina	uk	X	Lower middle income
Bulgaria	uk	X	Lower middle income
Croatia	uk	X	Upper middle income
Czech Republic	uk	X	Upper middle income
Estonia	na	X	Upper middle income
Georgia	x	X	Low income
Hungary	x	X	Upper middle income
Kazakhstan	x	X	Lower middle income

Kyrgyzstan	x		Low income
Latvia	x	X	Upper middle income
Lithuania	na	X	Upper middle income
Macedonia	uk	X	Lower middle income
Poland	uk	X	Upper middle income
Romania	x	X	Lower middle income
Russian Federation	x	X	Lower middle income
Slovakia			Upper middle income
Slovenia	na	X	High income: nonOECD
Tajikistan		X	Low income
Turkey	uk	X	Lower middle income
Turkmenistan	x	X	Lower middle income
Ukraine	x	X	Low income
Uzbekistan	x	X	Low income
Region: Latin America and the Caribbean			
Antigua and Barbuda	uk		Upper middle income
Argentina		X	Upper middle income
Bahamas	x	X	High income: nonOECD
Barbados	x	X	Upper middle income
Belize			Lower middle income
Bolivia	x	X	Lower middle income
Brazil	x	X	Upper middle income
Chile	x	X	Upper middle income
Colombia	x	X	Lower middle income
Costa Rica		X	Upper middle income
Cuba	na	X	Lower middle income
Dominica	uk		Upper middle income
Dominican Republic	x	X	Lower middle income
Ecuador	x	X	Lower middle income
El Salvador		X	Lower middle income
Grenada	uk		Upper middle income
Guatemala	x	X	Lower middle income
Guyana	x		Lower middle income
Haiti	uk		Low income
Honduras	x		Lower middle income
Jamaica			Lower middle income
Mexico	x	X	Upper middle income
Nicaragua	x	X	Low income
Panama	x	X	Upper middle income
Paraguay	x	X	Lower middle income
Peru	x	X	Lower middle income
Saint Kitts and Nevis	uk		Upper middle income
Saint Lucia	uk	X	Upper middle income
Saint Vincent and Grenadines	uk	X	Lower middle income
Suriname			Lower middle income

Trinidad and Tobago	x	X	Upper middle income
Uruguay	x	X	Upper middle income
Venezuela	x	X	Upper middle income
Region: Middle East and North Africa			
Algeria	na	X	Lower middle income
Bahrain	uk	X	High income: nonOECD
Cyprus	x	X	High income: nonOECD
Djibouti	uk		Lower middle income
Egypt	x	X	Lower middle income
Iran, Isl. Rep.	na	X	Lower middle income
Iraq	na	X	Lower middle income
Israel	x	X	High income: nonOECD
Jordan	na	X	Lower middle income
Kuwait	na	X	High income: nonOECD
Lebanon	x	X	Upper middle income
Libyan Arab Jamahiriya	na		Upper middle income
Malta	x	X	Upper middle income
Morocco	na	X	Lower middle income
Oman	x	X	Upper middle income
Qatar	uk	X	High income: nonOECD
Saudi Arabia	na	X	Upper middle income
Syrian Arab Republic	na	X	Lower middle income
Tunisia	uk	X	Lower middle income
United Arab Emirates	x	X	High income: nonOECD
Yemen	x	X	Low income
Region: North America			
Canada		X	High income: OECD
USA	x	X	High income: OECD
Region: South Asia			
Bangladesh	x	X	Low income
Afghanistan	na		Low income
Bhutan	uk		Low income
Maldives	na	X	Lower middle income
India	x	X	Low income
Nepal	uk	X	Low income
Pakistan	x	X	Low income
Sri Lanka		X	Lower middle income
Region: Sub-Saharan Africa			
Angola			Low income
Benin	uk		Low income
Botswana		X	Upper middle income
Burkina Faso		X	Low income
Burundi			Low income
Cameroon		X	Low income
Cape Verde	na	X	Lower middle income
Central African Rep.			Low income

Chad			Low income
Comoros	uk		Low income
Congo			Low income
Cote D'Ivorie	uk	X	Low income
Equatorial Guinea	uk		Low income
Eritrea			Low income
Ethiopia			Low income
Gabon		X	Upper middle income
Gambia			Low income
Ghana	x	X	Low income
Guinea		X	Low income
Guinea-Bissau			Low income
Kenya	x	X	Low income
Lesotho	uk		Low income
Liberia	uk		Low income
Madagascar		X	Low income
Malawi			Low income
Mali	uk	X	Low income
Mauritania		X	Low income
Mauritius	x	X	Upper middle income
Mozambique	uk		Low income
Namibia		X	Lower middle income
Niger	na		Low income
Nigeria	x	X	Low income
Rwanda			Low income
Sao Tome and Principe			Low income
Senegal		X	Low income
Seychelles	uk		Upper middle income
Sierra Leone	uk		Low income
Somalia	na		Low income
South Africa	na	X	Lower middle income
Sudan	na	X	Low income
Swaziland			Lower middle income
Tanzania, United Republic of	x	X	Low income
Togo			Low income
Uganda		X	Low income
Zambia	x	X	Low income
Zimbabwe	x		Low income
Region: Western Europe			
Andorra	uk	X	High income: nonOECD
Austria		X	High income: OECD
Belgium	x	X	High income: OECD
Denmark	na	X	High income: OECD
Finland	na	X	High income: OECD
France	x	X	High income: OECD

Germany	x	X	High income: OECD
Greece	x	X	High income: OECD
Iceland	na	X	High income: OECD
Ireland	x	X	High income: OECD
Italy	na	X	High income: OECD
Luxembourg	na	X	High income: OECD
Monaco	uk		High income: nonOECD
Netherlands	x	X	High income: OECD
Norway	na	X	High income: OECD
Portugal	x	X	High income: OECD
San Marino	uk		High income: nonOECD
Spain		X	High income: OECD
Sweden	x	X	High income: OECD
Switzerland		X	High income: OECD
UK		X	High income: OECD
Region: Other			
Cook Islands	x	X	
East Timor			
Nauru			
Niue	uk		
Tuvalu			

Source: UICC GLOBALink – http://www.globalink.org/tccp/.
Data refer to regulations by the central government only.
Notes: uk = unknown, na = not applicable.

Chapter 7

Territorial Smoking Restrictions

Introduction

Another policy to reduce smoking, besides advertising bans and taxation of tobacco products, deals with restrictions on smoking in public places and youth access to tobacco. The primary motives behind these policies relate to the rights of non-smokers who are affected by second-hand smoke. These policies increase the indirect costs of smoking by making smoking more inconvenient. These restrictions are also referred to as environmental smoking restrictions.

Territorial Anti-Smoking Policies

While initially workplace restrictions were due to concerns about fire safety and food contamination, in the seventies indoor air quality became a concern (Chaloupka and Saffer 1988). This policy arose primarily from knowledge about the adverse effects of second-hand smoke (that is effects on the non-smoker). Another thrust behind the prevalence of workplace bans has been the economic incentives from insurance companies. Insurance companies, due to fire hazards of smoking and the costs on non-smokers, now routinely charge higher premiums to establishments without any designated smoking areas. These restrictions also protect other consumers (for example designated non-smoking areas in restaurants) and workers (for example smoking bans on airplanes). By imposing restrictions on where the smokers can smoke, policy makers are implicitly trying to raise the costs of smoking.

Alciati et al. (1998) developed a rating system regarding the strength of laws restricting youth access to tobacco in the USA. They conclude that while all states in US have laws restricting youth access to tobacco, there were significant variations across states. Regulations that allowed state-level laws to pre-empt local laws regarding tobacco access were becoming quite prevalent.[1] Woollery, Asma and Sharp (2000) note the lack of territorial restrictions on a global scale. Clean indoor air policies were found prevalent in high-income nations, but were largely lacking in middle-income and low-income nations. However, some of this is being remedied with international treaties, like the Framework Convention on Tobacco Control (see Chapter 9 for more details).

---

1 See Jacobson and Wasserman (1997) for case studies of tobacco control laws in a number of individual states in the U.S.

Evidence Regarding the Effectiveness of Territorial Restrictions

Significant work on the effectiveness of workplace smoking restrictions in the USA is due to Chaloupka and associates. Chaloupka and Saffer (1988) used data on US states to determine the effect of workplace smoking restrictions on cigarette consumption. They find that cigarette demand in a state had a negative impact on the state's ability to legislate clean air restrictions. Even in states that enacted such laws, they were found to not have a significant negative impact on cigarette demand.

A detailed study of the effects of regulation on teenage smoking was by Chaloupka and Wechsler (1995). This research was based on survey data from more than 17,500 college students in the USA. A wide range of smoking regulations aimed at reducing teenage smoking were examined in this study. Chaloupka and Wechsler (1995) found that strong restrictions on smoking in public places (for example restrictions on smoking in restaurants) significantly reduced smoking participation rates among teenagers. However, they found that limits on availability of cigarettes to youth had little impact on the smoking behavior of college students (Chaloupka, 1995).

Internationally, we found stronger evidence pointing to the effectiveness of workplace smoking bans. For example, Bardsley and Olekalns (1999) have found workplace smoking bans to be effective deterrents to smoking in the case of Australia. This study supports earlier findings regarding workplace smoking restrictions for Australia by Wakefield et al. (1992). Wakefield et al.'s survey examined total and partial workplace smoking bans and found both to be effective in reducing smoking in South Australia. They found no change in smoking behavior of workers who did not face any workplace smoking restrictions. Further, Borland et al. (1991) found workplace bans effective in the case of Telecom Australia. Brenner and Mielck (1992) surveyed individuals in the Federal Republic of Germany during 1987 and found that workplace smoking bans were particularly effective in reducing smoking among German females.

Some researchers have examined the effectiveness of territorial smoking bans using composite indexes of regulation (Lanoie and Leclair (1998) and Laugesen and Meads (1991)). In such cases it is not possible to discern the effectiveness of any one type of measure. Since workplace restrictions are particularly sensitive to the location, one would need data at the micro level to discern the effectiveness of these restrictions. For example, potential smokers have less freedom in avoiding some no-smoking areas than others. A smoker can avoid eating at a no smoking restaurant, but has less freedom in avoiding his/her no smoking workplace. Are smoking restrictions imposed in restaurants more effective than those imposed in offices? These kinds of differences are difficult to discern with aggregated data sets. In spite of these limitations, the evidence regarding the effectiveness of workplace smoking restrictions seems more clear than in the case of advertising bans and health warnings.

The findings in the literature on the effectiveness of territorial restrictions are summarized in Table 7.1.

Table 7.1 Effectiveness of territorial and other smoking restrictions

Study	*Data*	*Effectiveness of restrictions in reducing smoking*
	US studies: using aggregate data	
Goel and Nelson (2005)	US, annual state-level, 1997	Indoor smoking restrictions effective at reducing smokeless tobacco use in adults, but ineffective at reducing cigarette prevalence (*)
Sung et al. (1994)	US, annual state-level, 1967–1990	Local regulations effective in reducing smoking (*)
	US studies: using micro data	
Chaloupka and Wechsler (1995)	US, survey of college students	Bans on smoking in public places effective in reducing teenage smoking
Czart et al. (2001)	US, college students, 1997	Comprehensive geographic restrictions reduce smoking; bans on cigarette sales increase smoking
	International studies: using aggregate data	
Bardsley and Olekalns (1999)	Australia, annual, 1962/63–1995/96	Workplace smoking bans and health warnings reduce consumption
	International studies: using micro data	
Borland, Owen and Hocking (1991)	Australia, Telecom Australia employees	Workplace smoking bans effective in reducing smoking
Brenner and Mielck (1992)	The Federal Republic of Germany, individuals, 1987	Workplace smoking bans effective in reducing smoking, especially among women
Lewit et al. (1997)	USA, Canada, school students, 1990, 1992	Policies limiting minors = access to tobacco and tobacco education reduce smoking; effect of geographic smoking restrictions insignificant
Stephens et al. (1997)	Canada, household data	Smoking bylaws effective at reducing smoking and even more effective in conjunction with higher cigarette prices
Wakefield et al. (1992)	Australia, individuals, 1989	Workplace smoking bans effective in reducing smoking

Note: (*) denotes that the study uses an index of regulation. See also Goel and Nelson (2006).

A meta-analysis of evidence from Australia, Canada, Germany and the USA was conducted by Fichtenberg and Glantz (2002). The authors find support for the effectiveness of smoke-free workplaces, both in their impacts on smokers and on non-smokers.

Additional Evidence on the Effectiveness of Territorial Smoking Restrictions

We present empirical estimates on the effectiveness of tobacco restrictions from Goel and Nelson (2005). These results, based on state-level US data for 1997, examine the effectiveness of geographic restrictions on both smoking- and smokeless tobacco use. Further, the results examine the effectiveness of these restrictions for adults as well as for youth. The estimated equations posit the prevalence of a tobacco type (that is cigarettes or smokeless tobacco for adults or youth) to be functions of own tax (to proxy for the price), consumer income, advertising and territorial restrictions. Three types of territorial restrictions are considered: i) indoor state-level restrictions on smoking including limits on smoking in workplaces, public places and common educational or health places (indoor restrictions); ii) age restrictions on sale of tobacco products to minors (age limits); and iii) restrictions on minor's access to tobacco products including restrictions on vending machines and other marketing restrictions (minor access). One should, however, keep in mind that in spite of the rich detail on various restrictions at the state-level, some institutional aspects of regulation are not prone to empirical interpretation.

Details about the variable definitions and the data sources (primarily, the Centers for Disease Control and Prevention) are presented in Table 7.2. The estimation results, based on ordinary least squares, are given in Table 7.3. The determinants on smoking prevalence are in columns two and three (for adults and youth, respectively), while the last two columns report results for the determinants of smokeless tobacco prevalence.

Overall the fit of the regressions explaining smokeless tobacco prevalence is better than that of cigarette use. However, the F-value is statistically significant in

Table 7.2 Data definitions and sources

Variable	*Definition*	*Source*
Adult smoking prevalence	Cigarette smoking among adults aged 18 and older, 1997; Smokeless tobacco use among adults aged 18+, 1995–1996 (% of adult population)	CDC (1999)
Youth smoking prevalence	Cigarette smoking among youth, grades 9–12, 1997; Smokeless tobacco use among youth, grades 9–12, 1997 (past month) (% of youth population)	CDC (1999)
Income	Per capita state income (US$)	BEA
Cigarette tax	Federal and state cigarette taxes (% of retail price)	CDC (1999)
Smokeless tax	Smokeless tobacco tax (% of cost or price)	CDC (1999)
Advertising restrictions	State imposed advertising restrictions (yes = 1; no restrictions = 0)	CDC (1999)
Indoor restrictions	State-level indoor smoke free restrictions on government worksites, private worksites, restaurants, day care centers, home-based day care (range: 0–5; with 0 = no restrictions)	CDC (1999)
Minor access	Restrictions for minors to purchase, possess, use tobacco products. Restrictions on vending machines, signage, licensure (range: 0–6; with 0 = no restrictions)	CDC (1999)
Age limits	Minimum age for sale of tobacco to minors (years)	CDC (1999)

Note: BEA is Bureau of Economic Analysis; CDC is Centers for Disease Control and Prevention.

Source: Goel and Nelson (2005).

all cases. The effect of income is negative as expected, but statistically significant only in the case of smokeless use. Thus, lower income taxes are likely to reduce smokeless tobacco use, while not significantly affecting the demand for cigarettes. Higher cigarette taxes reduce smoking, especially among adults, whereas the effect of higher taxes on smokeless tobacco is not statistically significant. Advertising restrictions do not seem to be effective in either case. This (insignificance) might be plausible in the Internet age, where advertisements in cyberspace are not easily regulated. Of the territorial restrictions, indoor smoking restrictions seems effective for smokeless tobacco (both for adults and youth), while age limits seem to work in reducing the number of smokers, especially youth. Minor access restrictions do not seem to have an appreciable impact in either case. Thus, these findings stress that among the various geographic tobacco restrictions, they are not all created alike. Further, their effectiveness is sensitive to population demographics and tobacco types. From a policy perspective, all this raises red flags against blanket restrictions.

Table 7.3 Effectiveness of territorial tobacco use restrictions in the USA

Dependable variable	*Smoking prevalence*		*Smokeless tobacco prevalence*	
	Adults	**Youth**	**Adults**	**Youth**
Constant	27.88* (9.32)	275.28* (3.32)	10.42* (9.15)	72.53 (0.91)
Income	-0.000,01 (0.11)	-0.000,5 (1.56)	-0.000,3* (5.57)	-0.000,4# (1.89)
Cigarette tax	-0.12# (1.87)	0.000,4 (0.00)		
Smokeless tax			-0.01 (1.57)	-0.04 (0.93)
Advertising restrictions	0.65 (0.70)	-1.59 (0.63)	-0.24 (0.61)	0.04 (0.02)
Indoor restrictions	-0.23 (0.73)	-1.39 (1.51)	-0.36* (2.91)	-1.23* (2.02)
Minor access		0.50 (0.60)		0.85 (1.56)
Age limits		-12.51* (2.77)		-2.90 (0.66)
N	51	34	49	32
Adj. -R^2	0.08	0.22	0.58	0.37
F	2.06*	2.59*	17.53*	4.10*

Note: t-statistics are in parentheses. * denotes statistical significance at least at the 5% level. # denotes statistical significance at least at the 10% level.

Source: Goel and Nelson (2005).

Chapter Summary

This chapter has provided an overview of the literature on the effectiveness of territorial or geographic tobacco restrictions. These restrictions take various forms dealing with the consumption and sale of tobacco products. Some of these restrictions, such as restrictions on the sale to minors, are aimed at population subgroups. Generally, the literature reports that these restrictions are an effective tool in the fight against tobacco use (Fichtenberg and Glantz, 2002). This has important policy relevance as various jurisdictions currently are trying to move toward creating smoke-free spaces.

We also present empirical results from a recent study of US states. These results focus on tobacco types (cigarettes and smokeless tobacco), demographics (youth and adults) and various territorial restrictions. Three types of territorial restrictions are considered: i) indoor state-level restrictions on smoking including limits on smoking in workplaces, public places and common educational or health places; ii) age restrictions on sale of tobacco products to minors; and iii) restrictions on minor's access to tobacco products including restrictions on vending machines and other marketing restrictions. Of the territorial restrictions, indoor smoking restrictions seem effective for smokeless tobacco (both for adults and youth), while age limits seem to work in reducing the number of smokers, especially youth. Minor access restrictions do not seem to have an appreciable impact in either case. Viewed as a whole, these findings stress that among the various geographic tobacco restrictions, they are not all created alike. The review of the literature reveals that territorial restrictions were effective in reducing smoking, especially in the case of USA. Internationally, workplace smoking bans seem to be effective. There is need, however, for studies based on data from developing nations and territorial smoking restrictions directed at population subgroups such as youth. This need has also been recognized in other studies (Woollery, Asma and Sharp, 2000). Further, the effectiveness of currently popular jurisdiction-wide bans (such as some localities banning smoking in all public places) will only be determined over time. Finally, as better data for the USA and information for other countries become available, further light can be shed on some of these aspects.

Chapter 8

Economics of Smoking Cessation

Introduction

The health benefits to people who stop smoking include lower risk of cancer, coronary heart disease, lower risk of adverse reproductive outcomes, and increased life expectancy.[1] Smoking cessation policies run a wide range, including subsidies or rewards for not smoking or for treatment, education, counseling (quit lines) and the provision of anti-smoking drugs (for example nicotine replacement therapies). While governments historically have been involved in smoking cessation initiatives, escalating insurance costs have more recently prompted private firms to also promote smoking control among their own employees. The importance of smoking cessation policies as an integral part of comprehensive strategies to reduce tobacco use has also been recognized by international bodies such as the World Health Organization.[2]

Tobacco control strategies aim to focus on two different constituencies. One set of strategies is geared towards potential smokers, to prevent smoking initiation. Other tobacco control programs seek to aid smokers to quit, or at least reduce smoking.[3] While the general nature all these strategies might be similar, there could be some qualitative differences. For instance, education-based policies might be best for preventing smoking initiation, while education coupled with subsidies (either direct or indirect) might be needed to induce smokers to quit.

An overview of the smoking trends, quit patterns, and death rates attributable to smoking for the USA in 2002 is presented in Table 8.1. In the year 2002, about half (52 percent) of the adult US smokers tried to quit smoking. The table also shows considerable variation in the smoking rates and quit rates across states. For example, smoking prevalence among adults ranged from a low of about 12 percent in Utah to a high of more than 30 percent in Kentucky. Not surprisingly, death rates (per 100,000 population) attributable to smoking are directly related to smoking prevalence with a correlation coefficient of 0.59 between the two variables. Quit attempts were highest in California, Rhode Island and Utah, but relatively low in Hawaii. These statistics

---

1 For further details see, CDC, *The Health Benefits of Smoking Cessation.* Atlanta, GA: U.S. Department of Health and Human Services, CDC, Center for Chronic Disease Prevention and Health Promotion, Office on Smoking and Health; 1990. DHHS Pub. No. (CDC) 90-8416, http://profiles.nlm.nih.gov/NN/B/B/C/T/. Also see CDC, *Women and Smoking: A Report of the Surgeon General.* Atlanta, GA: U.S. Department of Health and Human Services, CDC, National Center for Chronic Disease Prevention and Health Promotion, Office on Smoking and Health; 2001, http://www.cdc.gov/tobacco/sgr/sgr_forwomen/index.htm.

2 http://www.who.int/tobacco/resources/publications/tobacco_dependence/en/.

3 One might yet also classify under the latter, former smokers who have had a relapse.

Table 8.1 Smoking prevalence, quit patterns, and death rates in the USA, 2002

State	*Smoking prevalence (%)*	*Try to quit (%)*	*Smoking related death rates*	*State*	*Smoking prevalence (%)*	*Try to quit (%)*	*Smoking related death rates*
Alabama	24.4	50.9	168	Montana	21.3	45.0	155
Alaska	29.4	49.5	70	Nebraska	22.8	52.2	140
Arizona	23.5	50.5	124	Nevada	26.0	49.5	144
Arkansas	26.3	51.9	179	New Hampshire	23.2	56.7	131
California	16.4	62.3	107	New Jersey	19.1	55.2	124
Colorado	20.4	51.2	93	New Mexico	21.2	50.0	111
Connecticut	19.5	59.3	138	New York	22.4	58.0	128
Delaware	24.7	50.4	146	North Carolina	26.4	53.2	135
D.C.	20.4	58.9	131	North Dakota	21.5	47.1	136
Florida	22.1	48.0	165	Ohio	26.6	46.7	166
Georgia	23.3	55.4	122	Oklahoma	26.7	48.1	165
Hawaii	21.1	42.4	87	Oregon	22.4	52.5	139
Idaho	20.6	53.2	108	Pennsylvania	24.6	49.8	160
Illinois	22.9	50.1	146	Rhode Island	22.5	61.7	159
Indiana	27.7	52.4	165	South Carolina	26.6	53.6	143
Iowa	23.1	46.6	157	South Dakota	22.6	52.0	140
Kansas	22.1	44.2	175	Tennessee	27.8	48.1	164
Kentucky	32.6	45.6	188	Texas	22.9	47.5	108
Louisiana	23.9	53.4	143	Utah	12.7	66.2	51
Maine	23.6	56.7	163	Vermont	21.2	51.8	133
Maryland	22.0	52.3	123	Virginia	24.6	50.5	123
Massachusetts	19.0	56.0	141	Washington	21.5	52.7	125
Michigan	24.2	56.1	146	West Virginia	28.4	43.5	212
Minnesota	21.7	53.1	110	Wisconsin	23.4	51.7	143
Mississippi	27.4	53.9	172	Wyoming	23.7	53.9	146
Missouri	26.6	44.5	179	**National**	**23.1**	**52.0**	**136**

Source: http://www.cdc.gov/sustainingstates, Table 1, and authors' calculations. Death rates are per 100,000 population.

suggest that policy makers, especially at the national level, should take into account the different behaviors across states when formulating policy.

Due to the habit-forming nature of nicotine, smokers become dependent or addicted to cigarettes and most of the smokers who try to quit are unsuccessful (see Chaloupka and Tauras 2004). Nicotine replacement therapy (NRT) is a broad term used for products that can be used for short periods to wean smokers away from cigarettes. Examples of NRT's include gum, patches, inhalers, and so on. Some of these products have been available in the USA without a prescription since the mid-nineties, while others still require a physician's prescription. The relative success of these products is unclear.[4]

Table 8.2 presents information on the relative costs of cigarettes and NRTs (including gum and patches) for various countries for 1996 (most recent data available). The annual cigarette costs were the highest in Australia (US$1,200 per year) and the lowest in Indonesia (US$38 per year).[5] Given the relative geographic proximity of these two nations, the cost difference was especially pronounced—the cost in Australia was more than 30 times the cost in Indonesia. Considerable variation in the costs of NRTs was evident across countries as well. For example, the cost of 3-month treatment of gum NRTs ranges from a figure as low as US$127 in Greece to over US$1,000 in Japan.[6] Further, between the two NRT products, one product was not consistently cheaper across nations. The relative costs of patches versus gum do not show a clear pattern across nations.[7] In some cases cigarette costs were lower than those of cessation products, while in other cases the reverse was true.

The price differences in NRT products across nations seem large enough to promote international trade – both legal and illegal. While the smuggling of tobacco products, primarily cigarettes, has received attention in the literature (see Chapter 4), the international trading in NRT products does not seem to have appeared on the radar screens of researchers and policymakers. It remains to be seen whether the recent global agreements such as the FCTC (Framework Convention on Tobacco Control) will bring greater cost parity, especially among the signatory nations.

The Related Literature

The literature on the success of NRT strategies is slowly beginning to emerge, although little is known about the success in nations outside the USA. Such information is important for policy purposes and for resource allocation.

Chaloupka and Tauras (2004) use pooled cross-sectional data for 50 metropolitan US markets between 1994 and 2002 to examine the impact of nicotine replacement therapies on cigarette demand. They find that NRT is a substitute for cigarettes (the cross-price elasticity between the two was found to be 0.38) and that the elasticity of cigarette demand with respect to NRT sales is -0.06. An earlier study by the same two authors (Tauras and Chaloupka, 2003) covered a different period and focused on the estimation of the demand for NRT products. The authors found the demand for NRTs to be negatively sloped and, like the later study, that cigarettes and NRTs were substitutes. The own-price elasticity of demand for NicoDerm CQ was found to be -2.33 and that for Nicorette was -2.46, implying that both products were quite

---

4 Hughes et al. (2003) performed a meta-analysis of the effectiveness of OTC NRT products and found their effectiveness rates to be similar to those of the prescription NRTs.

5 These differences reflect both price differences between two countries as well as differences in the average annual consumption of tobacco. Per capita annual consumption is generally lower in countries at lower stage of development (see Table 1.3 in Chapter 1).

6 A three-month treatment of NRT is generally recommended by product suppliers.

7 Information on the extent and nature of smoking cessation subsidies across nations is not readily available.

Table 8.2 Costs of cigarettes and NRTs (1996; US dollars)

Countries	*Cost of cigarettes (annual)*	*Cost of NRTs (3 months)*	
		Gum	**Patches**
Argentina	191	358	316
Australia	1,200	168	200–356
Austria	451	242	341–351
Belgium	881	186	367–385
Brazil	135	–	492–517
Canada	613	248–518	328–377
Czech Republic	52	176	199
Finland	652	144–162	155–169
France	447	330	327–330
Germany	664	345	282–316
Greece	463	127–144	65–231
Hong Kong	211	270	352
Hungary	128	151	–
Indonesia	38	273	–
Ireland	339	253	260 - 264
Italy	339	193–214	256 - 275
Japan	502	976–1,010	–
Malaysia	127	287	271
Mexico	61	–	179–257
Netherlands	474	228 - 287	271–288
New Zealand	686	229	182–192
Norway	358	218	266–271
Poland	84	–	195
Portugal	301	272	247–348
Singapore	475	–	240
South Africa	151	193	215–217
Spain	233	140–193	263–359
Thailand	64	222	412
United Kingdom	770	163–175	213–235
United States	479	441–745	400–472

Source: Novotny et al. (2000, p. 298)

sensitive to price changes. An important policy implication of these elasticities is that as prices of NRTs fall, due to increased competition or government intervention, the usage of NRT products would disproportionately increase. Further, the cross-price elasticities with respect to cigarettes were quite similar for both products: 0.77 in the case of NicoDerm CQ and 0.76 for Nicorette. Thus, consumers tended to view both products as substitutes for cigarettes and the order of magnitude was roughly the same.

Novotny et al. (2000) note the low usage of NRT's in middle- and low-income nations. This is despite the fact that the prices of NRT products in most nations were lower than those in the USA (see Table 8.2). The authors cite governmental sales restrictions and lack of awareness as the causes behind the low NRT usage.

New Evidence on the Determinants of Smoker Quit Rates

Having reviewed the literature, we now turn to a presentation of empirical results. We present here some recent results from Goel (forthcoming) regarding the determinants of quit behavior in the USA. We focus on the important question of determinants of quit behavior: what are the key factors inducing smokers to quit smoking? According to standard economic theory, rational individuals would balance the relative costs and benefits of (smoking and) quitting smoking (Chaloupka, 1991; Harris and Harris, 1996). Other things being equal, higher cigarette prices, higher medical costs, greater restrictions on smoking, are likely to induce people to quit smoking. A more educated population is also better able to comprehend the long term health effects of smoking and thus would be more likely to quit.[8] Further, wealthier individuals have greater resources at their disposal to quit smoking. Major tobacco producing states might also affect attempts to quit smoking in significant ways. Aside from the relatively low cigarette taxes typically observed in these states the social stigma associated with tobacco consumption might be lower than in other states where the tobacco industry is less important.[9]

We take all these factors into account in the econometric investigation of the determinants of smoking cessation. Specifically, we estimate an equation that takes the following form:

$$QUITsmoke_i = f(CigPrice_i, Education_i, Income_i, MedicalCost_i, POLICYwork_i, POLICYhome_i, Control_i, Producer) \quad (1)$$
$$i = 1\ldots, 51.$$

QUITsmoke is the percent of smokers who tried to quit smoking in the *i*th U.S. state in 2002. Strictly speaking, *QUITsmoke* captures current smokers who smoked every day and tried to quit for one day or longer (see CDC for details). *CigPrice* is the retail, tax-inclusive price per 20th-pack of cigarettes in the state, *Education* is the percentage of population over 25 with at least a high school diploma. *Income* is per capita state income. *MedicalCost* denotes smoking attributable (lost) productivity and medical costs. *POLICYhome* and *POLICYwork* are, respectively, smoking restrictions at home and at work.[10] *Producer* is a binary variable that identifies the six major tobacco producing states in the United States (Georgia, Kentucky, North Carolina, South Carolina, Tennessee and Virginia) (Capehart, 2004), to see whether

8 On the other hand, a more educated population might not initiate smoking in the first place.

9 Nicotine replacement therapies were not considered in the model due to lack of data.

10 The policy variables are based on responses to surveys: POLICYwork includes responses where smoking at work was not allowed in indoor public areas and work areas. POLICYhome deals with instances where smoking was banned in the respondents' homes. See CDC, www.cdc.gov/tobacco/datahighlights/.

smokers in these states behaved somewhat differently from other smokers. In our analysis the price of cigarettes signifies the direct costs of smoking, while *MedCost* and nonsmoking policies (*POLICYhome* and *POLICYwork*) can be seen as capturing indirect smoking costs. *Control* denotes state-level expenditures on tobacco control initiatives.

Data for this study comprise state-level observations for all 50 states in the USA and the District of Columbia for the year 2002. Details about the variables used, data sources and summary statistics are provided in Table 8.3. All equations were

Table 8.3 Variable definitions and data sources

Variable	*Definition - mean (std. dev.)*	*Source*
QUITsmoke	Smokers who tried to quit (percent, by state) 51.9 (4.91)	www.cdc.gov/tobacco/datahighlights/
POLICYwork	People protected by nonsmoking policies at work (percent, by state) 68.6 (6.46)	www.cdc.gov/tobacco/datahighlights/
POLICYhome	People protected by nonsmoking policies at home (percent, by state) 59.8 (7.41)	www.cdc.gov/tobacco/datahighlights/
CigPrice	Price per pack of cigarettes (US$/ pack, by state) 3.70 (0.58)	www.cdc.gov/tobacco/datahighlights/
Control	Per capita tobacco control expenditures (US$, by state) 3.94 (3.63)	http://www.cdc.gov/tobacco/statehi/html_2002/tables.htm
MedicalCost	Smoking attributable medical and productivity costs (US$/ pack, by state) 8.61 (2.47)	www.cdc.gov/tobacco/datahighlights/
TotalCost	Total smoking costs = (Price + MedCost) (US$/ pack, by state) 12.31 (2.88)	www.cdc.gov/tobacco/datahighlights/
Education	Population over 25 with high school or more education (percent, by state) 86.46 (3.62)	*Statistical Abstract of the US*
Income	Per capita disposable income (current US$, by state) 29,018.86 (4,209.91)	*Statistical Abstract of the US*
Producer	Binary variable which equals 1 for the six major tobacco producing states (GA, KY, NC, SC, TN, VA); and 0 otherwise 0.12 (0.32)	

Note: The data are for the year 2002, or the closest year available.

estimated in OLS and heteroscedasticity-consistent standard errors are reported in Table 8.4.

The fit of all regressions when judged by the adjusted R^2 and the F-statistic is considered reasonable considering that the study is cross-sectional for 2002. The F-value is statistically significant at the 5 percent level in all of the models estimated. The key results are:

- From the positive and statistically significant coefficient on *CigPrice*, it is evident that higher cigarette prices induce greater quitting attempts. For instance, a US$1 increase in the per-pack price of cigarettes (about a 25 percent increase over the sample mean per-pack cigarette price of US$3.70) would

Table 8.4 Costs of smoking and attempts to quit smoking in the USA

	(Dependent variable: QUITsmoke)			
CigPrice	1.64 (1.24)	3.80** (1.24)		
Education	−0.30 (0.19)	−0.05 (0.29)	−0.09 (0.27)	−0.08 (0.26)
Income	0.0003 (0.0002)	0.0001 (0.0003)	0.0003 (0.0002)	0.0002 (0.0002)
MedicalCost			0.37 (0.28)	
TotalCost				0.40 (0.24)
POLICYwork	0.11 (0.11)			
POLICYhome	0.23** (0.09)			
Control		−0.40 (0.25)		
Producer	1.94 (1.35)	0.62 (1.76)		
Adjusted R^2	0.27	0.14	0.10	0.11
F-value	4.1**	2.9**	2.8**	3.1**
N	51	48	51	51

Notes: See Table 8.3 for variable definitions.

All equations included a constant term. The results for the constant term are not reported but are available upon request. The figures in parentheses are heteroscedasticity-consistent standard errors.

** denotes statistical significance at least at the 5 percent level.

Source: Goel (forthcoming) and authors' calculations.

lead to about a 3.8 percent increase in the smokers who try to quit.[11] The finding of a price effect that is statistically significant is in contrast to those for Australia using micro-level data (Kidd and Hopkins, 2004).

- Greater education (Education) lowers the quit attempts, although the relevant coefficient is not statistically significant.
- The effect of greater personal income (Income) on quit attempts does not appear to be statistically significant implying that the income level does not seem to play a key role. The statistical insignificance of the income variable has also generally been found in other studies of smoking quitting behavior (Hsieh, 1998; Keeler et al., 1999).
- Higher medical cost (*MedicalCost*) makes quitting smoking more likely, however, the resulting coefficient is statistically insignificant. It might be the case that medical costs might be partially borne only indirectly by some individuals (that is individuals with insurance) and they might not directly feel the increase in these costs, at least not in the short run.
- In contrast, when the cost of smoking is defined more broadly to include both the medical costs and the price of cigarettes (*TotalCost*), then the results indicate that higher costs measured in this way leads to more quit attempts. The coefficient on the *TotalCost* variable is statistically significant at conventional levels.
- More restrictive smoking policies at home (*POLICYhome*) seem to induce greater quitting attempts and the resulting coefficient is statistically significant.
- Similarly, anti-smoking restrictions in the workplace (*POLICYwork*) do not seem to have an appreciable impact on quit attempts. The ineffectiveness of workplace restrictions has been found elsewhere (Hammar and Carlsson, 2005).
- The effects of state expenditures on tobacco control (*Control*) do not seem to significantly affect cessation behavior. It might be the case that a large part of these expenditures might be directed at lower, not necessarily stopping, tobacco use.
- Finally, the binary variable identifying the six major tobacco-producing states (*Producer*) consistently show that these states do not induce greater quit attempts.

One should bear in mind, however, that the results presented in this section are based on data from one country (that is the United States). Future research will enlighten us whether these findings hold in the case of other nations (and other time periods).

11 It might be the case that a number of quit attempts turn out to be unsuccessful over time (Keeler et al., 1999). It is also possible that some of the cigarette smokers might be switching to other lower-priced tobacco products (Laxminarayan and Deolalikar, 2004).

Chapter Summary

This chapter has focused on the economics of smoking cessation. Over half of all current (2002) adult smokers have attempted to quit, yet it is difficult to do given the addictive nature of the product. Nicotine replacement therapies have given smokers an additional treatment approach to stop smoking. These products can be used to supplement more traditional methods such as individual self-help materials and group counseling. The literature on the effectiveness of these strategies is still in its infancy but recent research has shown the NRTs as part of a comprehensive treatment plan can be effective in helping smokers quit. However, recent evidence summarized in this chapter also indicates that the demand for NRT products is sensitive to price. NRT products are quite expensive in many countries. If they are going to be used more widely among the smoking population, policy makers may have to look at strategies to lower the cost of these products.

This chapter also presented the empirical results from a recent study of quit behavior. It seems that higher cigarette prices remain the key instrument to induce quit attempts. In other words, the direct costs of smoking seem more important in quit decisions than the indirect costs. It is also evident that the territorial restrictions increase the costs of smoking by making it inconvenient to smoke, although the statistical significance of workplace restrictions is low.

The results show that the price of cigarettes is the primary thrust behind a smoker's decision to quit. A US$1 increase in the per-pack price of cigarettes would lead to about a 3.8 percent increase in the smokers who try to quit. The indirect costs due to territorial smoking restrictions and medical costs do not seem to significantly matter. For example, a US$10 increase in total cost of smoking (as defined in Table 8.3) would increase the percentage of smokers trying to quit by about 4 percent.

One implication of these results is that, many scholars argue, due to the relatively low price elasticity of cigarette demand (Chaloupka and Warner, 2000, and Goel and Nelson, 2006), the ability of policymakers to reduce smoking via higher cigarette taxes is rather limited and that non-price policies must be considered. The results of this study show that the price measures, rather than non-price smoking policies, hold promise in terms of inducing smoking quitting attempts. Thus, cigarette taxes remain a viable tobacco policy instrument.

Chapter 9

Comprehensive Tobacco Control Policies

Introduction

In recent years, governments in both the USA and elsewhere have implemented comprehensive smoking-reduction plans. These plans cover various price and non-price initiatives to combat smoking and have the advantage of eliminating or reducing redundancies and spillovers and creating synergies among the various initiatives that make up the overall policy. A comprehensive approach to tobacco control is rationalized on the basis that the decisions people make regarding the consumption of tobacco products are based on a complex set of factors. The factors include economic considerations (for example price, income), social influences (for example peer pressure, customs and religion, and the general societal views towards tobacco), the legal environment, and past consumption behavior (reflecting the addictive nature of most tobacco products). An effective tobacco control policy requires the coordinated implementation of multiple strategies that are informed by how individuals make decisions in this area.

Policy intervention can also take place from both the demand side and the supply side of the market for tobacco products. Here as well, with comprehensive policies there is less chance of individual policies working at cross-purposes. An example of conflicting tobacco control policies would be government subsidies to tobacco farmers on the one hand and restrictions on the sale and marketing of tobacco products on the other hand.

This chapter provides an overview of the current state of public policy regarding the comprehensive control of tobacco, both in the USA and internationally. In addition, what is known about the effectiveness of these policies is also summarized. Two noteworthy tobacco control initiatives that are comprehensive in nature are highlighted as part of this discussion. These include the Master Settlement Agreement (MSA) between tobacco companies and states in the United States in 1998 and the recent Framework Convention on Tobacco Control (FCTC) at the international level.

Comprehensive Tobacco Control Programs in the United States

Several U.S. states have been leaders in the development of comprehensive tobacco control programs over the latter part of the last century. These individual state programs have varied in terms of specific goals and outcomes and they have formed the basis for recommendations at the national level as to what constitutes best practices for the comprehensive tobacco control policy.

Four of these early state programs were the outcomes of voter initiatives, including California (1989); Massachusetts (1993), Arizona (1994), and Oregon (1996). Each of these programs was financed by increases in taxes on tobacco products with the revenues partially dedicated for tobacco control programs.[1] Two other state programs, in Minnesota (1975) and Maine (1997), were the result of legislative action and were also financed by increases in excise taxes on tobacco products.

A considerable number of studies have assessed the effectiveness of these state programs and the preponderance of the evidence suggests that they have been effective at reducing tobacco consumption and the prevalence of teenage smoking.[2] Notable are the results for programs in California and Massachusetts, both of which were extensive in scope and sustained over a number of years. For example, per capita tobacco consumption in Massachusetts declined by nearly 19 percent between 1992 (the year before their program was implemented) and 1996. In California the percentage reduction in per capita consumption was nearly 20 percent during a similar time period. These figures compare favorably to the 5 percent reduction in per capita consumption for the U.S. as a whole during this time period (Orzechowski and Walker, 2001). Based on the experiences in these states, the Center for Disease Control (CDC) published a set of guidelines to the states on *Best Practices for Comprehensive Tobacco Control Programs* in 1999 (CDC, 1999; Wakefield and Chaloupka, 2000).

The stated goals of the CDC *Best Practices* recommendations (CDC, 1999, pp. 374–375) are:

- Prevent initiation of tobacco use among young people;
- Promote quitting among adults and young people;
- Eliminating exposure to environmental territorial smoke;
- Identify and eliminate disparities among population groups.

To accomplish these goals the CDC recommends a tobacco control program consisting of nine components (CDC, 1999, *Fact Sheet*):

- Community programs to discourage smoking among adults and young people. Communities are taken here to include, but are not restricted to, social, civic, business, labor, religious organizations.
- Programs related to the understanding and prevention of chronic diseases such as cancer and heart disease.
- School programs to educate young people on the negative health consequences of tobacco consumption.
- Insuring that there are sufficient resources to enforce existing policies on tobacco control and educating the public about the importance of these policies.
- Counter-marketing to offset the marketing and promotional activities of the tobacco industry.

---

1 For a further description of these programs and a summary of the evidence on their effectiveness, see CDC (1999), Chapter 7, and Wakefield and Chaloupka (2000).

2 See Wakefield and Chaloupka (2000) for a review of this literature through the year 2000.

- Implementation of statewide programs along with community-based programs to insure some geographic uniformity of tobacco control policies.
- Programs to assist people to stop smoking.
- Policies set in place to regularly evaluate and assess the success of the various program to control tobacco and to make recommendations for policy improvement.
- Effective administration and management of existing tobacco control policy.[3]

The CDC has estimated for each state the lower- and upper-bound outlays that would be required to implement all the *Best Practices* program recommendations.[4] The per capita cost estimates vary from state to state depending upon the demographic characteristics of each state, smoking consumption and prevalence, and other factors. In 2002, for example, lower-bound estimates by the CDC ranged from under US$5 per capita (California, Florida, and Texas) to nearly US$15 per capita (Wyoming). There are sharing economies associated with some of the tobacco control programs (for example statewide training and infrastructure) so per capita costs tend to be somewhat lower in larger states according to CDC estimates.[5]

The CDC also calculates the actual amount of resources in each state that are allocated for comprehensive tobacco control from all sources, including state appropriations, federal funding, national organizations (for example, American Cancer Society) and other non-governmental sources (for example, Robert Wood Johnson Foundation). For 2001–2002 (latest data available), funding for tobacco control programs averaged approximately 58 percent of the recommended amount (low estimate) for the 50 states. Figure 9.1 displays the corresponding funding percentage for each state. The range is considerable, with Ohio tobacco control funding nearly three times the CDC recommended amount, while Tennessee funded only 5 percent of the recommended amount during this time period.

To gain further insight into the effectiveness of tobacco control funding in curtailing smoking a simple regression model is estimated with the change in smoking prevalence as the dependent variable and the average per capita funding for tobacco control in 2001–2002 as the right-hand-side explanatory variable. The model is estimated separately for adults and for youth using state-level data. For adults, the change in smoking prevalence is calculated over the 1998–2002 period for all 50 states. Comparable data for youth are much more restricted, both in terms of beginning and ending years that can be used for the analysis and in terms of the number of states with available data. For this group the change in smoking prevalence

---

3 For a further discussion of these policies see CDC (1999), Chapter 7, especially pages 374–376.

4 Centers for Disease Control and Prevention, State Tobacco Activities Tracking and Evaluation (STATE) System, http://www.cdc.gov/tobacco/statesystem.

5 Per capita cost estimates are authors calculations based on CDC (1999) data. The funding estimates reported by the CDC are based on state demographics and tobacco usage that existed in 1999.

was calculated over the 1997–2003 time period for 19 states.[6,7] The Ordinary Least Squares estimates are reported in Table 9.1.

The results for adults indicate that state tobacco control funding has had little effect on adult smoking prevalence during the time period under analysis (see the middle column of Table 9.1). The estimated coefficient on the variable is negative, although not statistically significant at conventional levels. In contrast, tobacco control funding has been effective at reducing smoking prevalence among the youth, at least for the 19 states where comparable data were available (see the right column of Table 9.1). The coefficient on the funding variable is positive and statistically significant at the 5 percent level. In particular, the result implies that an additional dollar per capita of tobacco control funding in a state will lead to reduction in youth smoking prevalence by a little less than one-half of 1 percent (0.41). For reference, the mean percentage reduction in youth smoking prevalence over this time period was 14.0 percent for the states included in the data set.[8]

These results are consistent with earlier work that has investigated the impact of state tobacco control expenditures on per capita cigarette sales. For example, Hu et al. (1995b) estimated the elasticity of such expenditures on per capita consumption to be -0.05 for California while Farrelly et al. (2003) estimated an elasticity of -0.0015 using a panel data set of the 50 states.

The United States of America Master Settlement Agreement

The landmark MSA between 46 states and U.S. tobacco companies in 1998 was a comprehensive deal between industry and government to combat tobacco use and to internalize the social costs of smoking (see Bulow and Klemperer, 1998; Capehart, 2001; and Viscusi, 2002, for details). Four states, Florida, Minnesota, Mississippi and Texas, independently reached agreements with tobacco companies. This Agreement, signed on November 16th, 1998, between States Attorneys General and cigarette manufacturers provided that the signatory states would receive US$206 billion over 25 years for health damages related to smoking. In addition, there were provisions in the agreement that prohibited targeting youth in advertising, funding for a counter advertising campaign, funding for tobacco research, marketing restrictions and the disbanding of tobacco industry lobbying organizations (Wilson, 1999).

While the long-term effects of this Agreement are still unfolding, there were some rather immediate consequences of the tobacco deal. For instance, cigarette prices jumped by 45 cents per pack the day the Agreement was reached to pay for

6 Source of all data: Centers for Disease Control and Prevention, State Tobacco Activities Tracking and Evaluation (STATE) System, http://www.cdc.gov/tobacco/statesystem.

7 Note that in both cases a positive number indicates that smoking prevalence in the state had fallen that percentage over the time period under analysis.

8 In preliminary analysis the change in real state tax rates on cigarettes were included in the adult and youth prevalence estimating equations as an additional right-hand-side variable. The results are generally consistent to what is reported in Table 9.1.

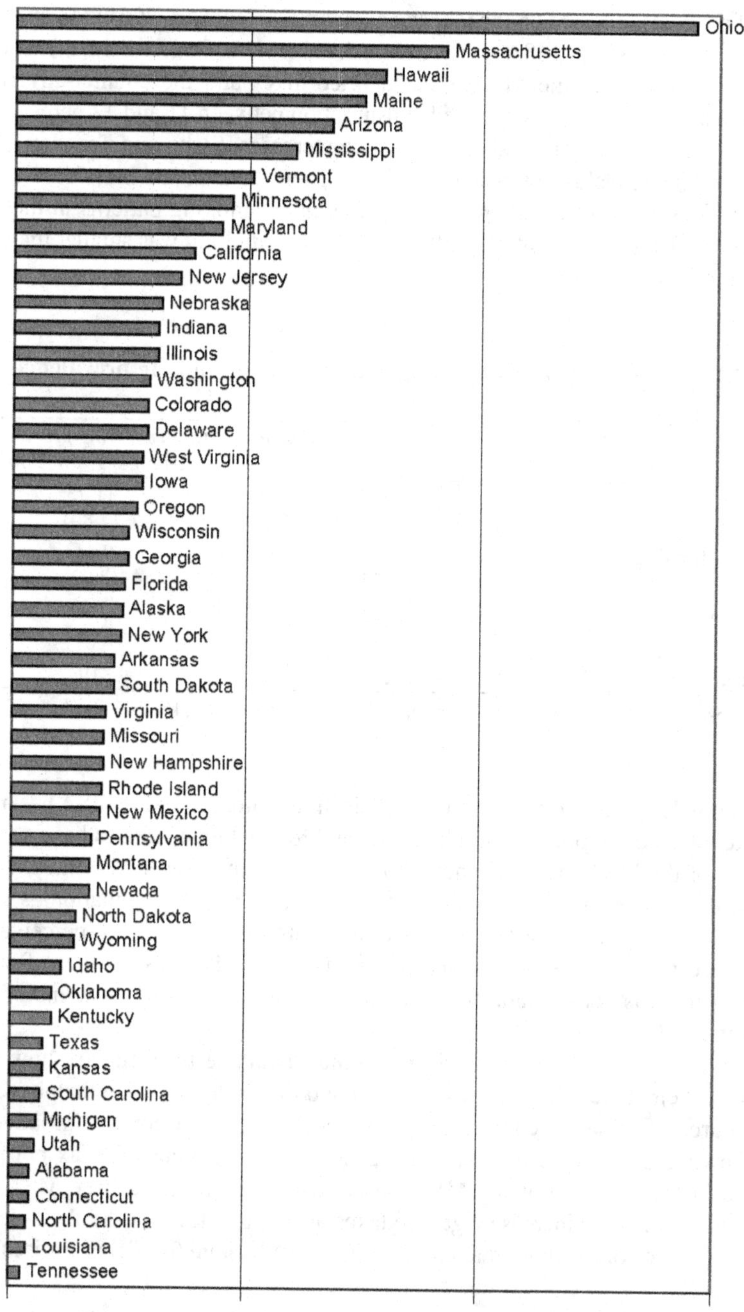

Figure 9.1 State funding as a percentage of CDC Best Practices recommendations

Source: Authors' estimates based on CDC data as reported at http://www.cdc.gov/tobacco/statesystem.

some of the costs imposed on the tobacco companies (Capehart, 2001).[9] In analyzing the early impact of the MSA using Massachusetts data Cutler and his associates (2002) concluded that the MSA-induced price hikes and the counter-advertising campaign at the federal level reduced consumption between 11 and 13 percent, with most of the reduction attributable to the price increases. Sloan and Trogdon (2004) reached similar conclusions using a national panel data set of individuals. More recently, Levy and Meara (2006) examined prenatal smoking patterns in the wake of the MSA. They found that the decline in prenatal smoking was smaller than what had been predicted.

Table 9.1 Tobacco control funding and change in smoking prevalence

	Adult smoking prevalence change: 1998–2002	*Youth smoking prevalence change: 1997–2003*
Constant	0.066	11.75
	(0.17)	(7.80)
Per capita funding	−0.051	0.41*
	(0.71)	(2.02)
R-squared	0.01	0.19
F-statistic	0.51	4.07*
Observations	50	19

Notes: Absolute value of t-statistic in parentheses, * = significant at the 5% level.

To our knowledge, there has been no analysis of the impact that the MSA has had on the state tobacco tax policy, including how and to what extent states have used the proceeds of the MSA to finance new tobacco control initiatives. Yet, the payments to individual states are substantial, even after controlling for population as shown in Table 9.2.[10] More interestingly, MSA payments are a substantial percentage of the tobacco tax revenues at the states-level. However, it is also evident from the table that there is considerable variation across individual states in terms of these payments.

We will leave it to others as data becomes available to document how states have used their share of the MSA settlement and the extent to which they have used the resources to finance comprehensive state-level tobacco control initiatives. In the following analysis we present evidence as to how state cigarette tax policy has changed in the years following MSA. In particular, did the states see MSA as an opportunity to further increase cigarette taxes at the state level or did they view the MSA as a source of revenues that could serve as a substitute for higher excise taxes?

9 Further, in the post-1998 period, there have been two increases in the federal tax on cigarettes (in 2000 and 2002).

10 Complete details of the payments to individual states are provided in the appendix.

Table 9.2 MSA payments to states: 2000–2004

Year	*Maximum (US$ per capita)*	*Mean (US$ per capita)*	*Minimum (US$ per capita)*	*MSA payments as % of state tax revenues on tobacco products*
2000	168	41	16	143
2001	74	29	12	95
2002	79	33	14	104
2003	79	29	13	70
2004	67	26	11	58

Sources: The Tax Burden on Tobacco and State Government Tax Collections (various years), U.S. Census Bureau.

Using pooled cross-sectional state-level data for five years, we report results from Goel and Nelson (2006b) where they examine the impact of the MSA on cigarette tax policy at the state level. In addressing this issue we control for political-economic influences on tax policy. Within that context, tax policy changes may be viewed as being influenced by economic (for example, budgetary considerations such as efforts to balance state budgets) and political (for example, lobbying by special interest groups) (Seiglie, 1990; Hettich and Winer, 1998).

In the case of tobacco tax policy several considerations may be relevant in determining how states may adjust their tobacco taxes after the MSA. First, policy makers may view this as an opportunity to raise taxes at lower political costs given the negative publicity tobacco companies faced from the legal proceedings leading up to the settlement (Sloan and Trodon, 2004). Second, states may also raise tobacco taxes as a means to offset expected revenue losses as sales decline from MSA-induced retail price hikes (Cutler et al., 2002). On the other hand, Cutler et al. also note that since MSA payments will exceed the expected loss in tobacco tax revenues states might conceivably lower tax rates and still achieve their revenue goals. Given all of this, it is unclear how state tax policy makers will respond to the MSA.

To address this empirically we posit a regression model where state-level cigarette taxes (*StateCigTAX*) is taken as a function of monetary payments from tobacco companies (*MSA*pc), state income (*INC*),[11] federal cigarette tax (*FedCigTAX*), the percentage of smokers (*Smokers*), whether the state signed the MSA with others or individually reached an agreement with tobacco companies (*Signed*), whether the state is a key tobacco producing state (*TobProducer*),[12] and the average cigarette tax rate in a state's geographic neighbors (*NeighborCigTAX*).[13] Thus, *TobProducer*

11 State income can be seen as capturing the budgetary compulsions of a state.

12 Six U.S. states, Georgia, Kentucky, North Carolina, South Carolina, Tennessee, and Virginia, produce the vast majority of tobacco in the country.

13 In the case of Florida, for instance, the *NeighborCigTAX* would be the average of the cigarette excise taxes in Alabama and Georgia.

and *Smokers* can be seen as capturing interest-group influences and *INC* serves as a proxy for budgetary compulsions.[14]

All these influences are considered in the empirical estimation. Formally, the estimated equation takes the following form, with subscripts i and t, respectively, denoting state and time.

$$StateCigTAX_{it} = f(MSApc_{it}, INC_{it}, FedCigTAX_t, Smokers_t, Signed_t, TobProducer_t, NeighborCigTAX_{it}) \quad (9.1)$$

$$i = 1, \ldots, 51$$
$$t = 2000, \ldots, 2004$$

The data for the study include annual state-level observations for all the states in the U.S. plus the District of Columbia.[15] All monetary data are expressed in nominal terms. The years (2000–2004) cover all the years in which MSA related payments have been received by states.

The estimation results are reported in Table 9.3. All equations were estimated using Ordinary Least Squares (OLS) and t-statistics based on robust standard errors are reported. The overall fit of all estimated equations is reasonable as shown by the statistically significant F-value and the adj. R^2 that is greater than or equal to 0.38 in all cases.

For all three variations of equation (1) reported in Table 9.3 the results for *MSApc* variable reveal that MSA payments have a positive effect on state cigarette taxes, suggesting that legislators viewed the time period following the MSA as an opportune time to hike cigarette taxes at low political cost. Policy makers may also consider tax increases and MSA payments as complementary in their goals to reduce smoking (and perhaps even generating additional revenues). The relevant coefficient is statistically significant in all three cases. Thus, beside price increases by tobacco companies to pay for the settlement, smokers have had to contend with higher taxes, especially in states that received greater MSA payments.

Besides providing the first formal look at the tax implications of MSA, the findings should have policy relevance. For example, if MSA payments and tax policy are complementary, then tobacco control can be seen as being strengthened following the Agreement. On the other hand, if tax policy and MSA turn out to be substitutes, then MSA payments could be seen as crowding out other tobacco control measures.

---

14 For further details on this regression set up and variable definitions and measurement see Goel and Nelson (2006b).

15 Since the four states (Florida, Minnesota, Mississippi, and Texas) that reached independent agreements with the tobacco companies are also included in the data set, a control variable (*Signed*) was included in the model to control for any provisions in the MSA that were unique to the 46 states that signed the deal as a group.

Table 9.3 State cigarette tax policy following MSA

	Dependent variable: State cigarette tax (StateCigTAX)		
MSApc	0.36* (3.0)	0.23* (2.2)	0.30* (2.8)
INC	0.003* (6.0)	0.003* (6.6)	0.002* (4.3)
FedCigTAX	3.50* (4.5)	3.32* (4.6)	2.36* (2.9)
Smokers	-3.31* (6.4)	-1.80* (3.6)	-2.66* (4.6)
Signed	26.79* (5.8)	27.90* (6.4)	19.98* (4.2)
TobProducer		-38.34* (9.2)	
NeighborCigTAX			0.35* (3.4)
F-value	32.09*	36.29*	32.55*
Adj. R^2	0.38	0.45	0.43
N	255	255	255

Notes: Variable definitions are provided in Table 9.1.
All equations included a constant term. The results for these are not reported, but are available upon request.
The figures in parentheses are (absolute values of) t-statistics based on robust standard errors. * denotes statistical significance at least at the 5% level.

Comprehensive Tobacco Control Programs Internationally

As noted in Chapter 1, non-price tobacco control polices vary widely among countries internationally. In this section we build on that analysis by constructing an index that measures the comprehensiveness of tobacco control polices for each country. We then use that index to describe the extent to which governments around the globe have adopted comprehensive polices to deter tobacco consumption. In constructing the index we restrict the analysis to focus only on non-price policies since pricing (tax) strategies are used to one degree or another by all governments to combat tobacco use.

The Comprehensive Policy Index (*Index*) that we use in this section is defined as follows:

$$Index = Advt + Sales + Terr + Warn, \tag{9.2}$$

where,

Advt = an index that measures the degree of advertising restrictions on tobacco products in a country. The index ranges from zero to three with larger numbers implying more comprehensive restrictions in this area.

Sales = an index that measures the restrictiveness of public policy with regard to the sale and distribution of tobacco products. The index ranges from zero to two with larger numbers implying more comprehensive restrictions in this area.

Terr = an index that measures the level of territorial restrictions on public smoking and/or "non-smokers" rights legislation. The index ranges from zero to three with larger numbers implying more comprehensive restrictions in this area.

Warn = an index that measures the degree the government mandates some form of health warning labels on tobacco products, restrictions on tar and nicotine content in cigarettes or requirements that these amounts must be displayed on the product packaging. The index ranges from zero to two with larger numbers implying more comprehensive restrictions in this area.

For a further description of the four indexes, sources of data, and caveats surrounding each measure, see Chapter 1 and Goel and Nelson (2004).

Index can range in value from zero to ten. A value of zero for the index implies that a country has no tobacco control policy in any of the areas listed above. In contrast, an index score of ten implies that the country has relatively comprehensive non-price tobacco control policies, at least in the four areas that comprise this index.

The Comprehensive Policy Index is calculated for all countries where data are available to construct the four sub indexes. In all, the *Index* was constructed for 105 countries for the year 2000 (latest available). The countries included in our data set vary considerably, both in terms of geographic location and with respect to stage of development. For all countries in the data set the mean value of the index was 6.82 with a standard deviation of 3.4. The index ranged in value from zero (six countries) to ten (27 countries).

Table 9.4 provides insights into how the comprehensiveness of non-price tobacco control policies varies by state of development. For ease of exposition, each country in the data set is classified into one of three categories in terms of how comprehensive their policies are: "High" (*Index* value of either nine or ten), "Middle" (*Index* value between four and eight inclusive), and "Low" (*Index* value of three or less). Countries are further grouped into four categories by stage of development using the 2003 World Bank classifications: "Low Income", "Lower-middle Income", "Upper-middle Income", and "High Income" (both OECD and non-OECD countries).

The results reveal the all but low-income countries have a reasonably high level of comprehensive non-price tobacco control policies. For example, of the 27 countries in the data set that are classified by The World Bank as high income, 17 countries (63 percent) had a Comprehensive Index score of nine or higher ("High" category). The remaining countries in this income grouping were classified in the "Middle" category (37 percent) as none of the 27 countries were in the "Low" category.

The results are generally similar for countries in both the upper- and lower-middle income stage of development (columns three and four in Table 9.4). More than half the countries in these income groupings were classified as having "High" comprehensive polices. A little more than 10 percent of the countries in these development categories, however, were classified as having a "Low" level of comprehensive tobacco control policies.

In contrast to the previous results the analysis reveals that over half (51 percent) of the countries in lowest development category do not have comprehensive tobacco control policies. This characterization does not fit all countries in that development category, however, as nearly one-quarter (22 percent) of the low-income countries in the data set ranked in this highest category with respect to comprehensive tobacco policy.[16] Nevertheless, the simple correlation between per capita 2000 GDP and the Comprehensive Policy Index is 0.32 which is statistically different from zero at better than the 1 percent significance level.

These findings are consistent with the conclusions of Jha and associates (2006) who use a somewhat different approach to measure the coverage of tobacco control policies for individual countries worldwide. They report a positive correlation between the comprehensiveness of tobacco control policies and stage of development and, similar to our analysis, they find wide variation among countries within each income group.

Some evidence regarding the effectiveness of multiple policies in the case of Canada is provided by Stephens et al. (1997). The authors find that while both higher cigarette prices (taxes) and smoking regulations reduced smoking prevalence in Canada, these policies were jointly more effective than separately.

Table 9.4 Non-price tobacco control policies and stage of development (number and percentage of countries in each category)

Level of comprehensive policies	*High income countries*	*Upper-middle income countries*	*Lower-middle income countries*	*Low income countries*
High (index 9–10)	17 (63%)	12 (63%)	14 (58%)	8 (22%)
Middle (index 4–8)	10 (37%)	5 (26%)	7 (29%)	9 (29%)
Low (index 0–3)	0	2 (11%)	3 (13%)	18 (51%)
Number of countries	27	19	24	35

Source: Authors' calculations based on data reported in *Tobacco Control Country Profiles* (2003).

16 When reviewing these results it should be kept in mind that the Comprehensive Policy Index was not calculated for countries that did not have sufficient data to calculate one or more of the four components that make up the Index. In all, 62 countries were excluded from the analysis, nearly three-quarters (45) of these were either low income or lower-middle income countries. As reported in Goel and Nelson (2004) many of these countries tend to have less stringent tobacco control policies generally. Thus, the lack of comprehensive tobacco control policies in low- and lower-middle income countries may be even greater than what is suggested by the data presented in Table 9.4.

Framework Convention on Tobacco Control

The Framework Convention on Tobacco Control (FCTC) is the world's first international health treaty aimed at getting signatory states to agree to impose a comprehensive set of non-price tobacco control measures to combat tobacco usage worldwide. It was instituted by the World Health Organization (WHO) and was entered into force in February 2005.[17]

A number of factors were behind the recognition of the need for a global tobacco control treaty. First, the ill-health effects of tobacco use are widespread enough to have affected most of the world. Second, the international dimensions of tobacco were becoming more prominent, especially on the supply side, including cross-border trade in tobacco products (both legal and illegal), transnational advertising and marketing, and so on.

A salient feature of the convention is that it emphasizes both tobacco demand reduction strategies and supply containment at a global scale. Specific measures signatory states are obligated to implement include:

- A comprehensive ban on tobacco advertising, promotion, and sponsorship;
- The adoption of health warnings and messages on tobacco products and outside packaging that must occupy 30 percent or more of the principle display areas;
- Measures to protect individuals from second-hand smoke;
- Measures that will effectively eliminate cross-border smuggling, illicit manufacturing, and counterfeiting of tobacco products.
  (*Source: World Health Organization, 2003.*)

The FCTC opened for signatures of nations on June 16, 2003 in Geneva, Switzerland. Until June 2004, it remained open for signatures at the United Nations Headquarters in New York. States that have signed the Convention have indicated that they will strive in good faith to ratify it and have committed themselves not to undermine it. Nations that did not sign the FCTC may now become a party to the treaty through accession. As of February 2007, 168 countries have signed the agreement and 144 countries have ratified the treaty. An updated list of parties to the agreement can be found at the World Health Organization website http://www.who.int/tobacco/framework/countrylist/en/index.html.

It is unclear at this point whether (and how quickly) the goals of the Treaty will be realized once it comes into force. The effectiveness will depend upon socio-economic factors as well as the political climate in individual nations. In some other instances, however, there is some evidence that comprehensive smoking control policies work better than individual programs at reducing tobacco use (see Farrelly et al. (2003) for evidence from the USA and Stephens et al. (1997) for evidence from Canada).

17 http://www.who.int/tobacco/framework/background/en/print.html.

Chapter Summary

Individual tobacco control policies, mainly price-based policies, have been popular with policy makers across the world for decades. Yet recent research suggests that consumption decisions on tobacco are based on a complex set of factors that include economic considerations, social and cultural influences, the legal environment, and past consumption behavior. Therefore, an effective tobacco control policy requires the coordinated implementation of multiple initiatives to influence individual to consume tobacco products.

This chapter provides a summary of the current state of public policy regarding the comprehensive control of tobacco, both in the U.S. and internationally. A considerable number of studies have assessed the effectiveness of US state programs, most notably in California and Massachusetts. These studies have concluded that these comprehensive strategies have been effective at reducing tobacco consumption and the prevalence of teenage smoking. Based on the experiences in these states the CDC published a set of guidelines to the states on *Best Practices for Comprehensive Tobacco Control Programs*.

Evidence presented in this chapter revealed that current levels of tobacco control spending across all the states has had little effect on adult smoking prevalence. In contrast, the evidence suggests that tobacco control funding has been effective at reducing smoking prevalence among the youth.

Recently, two prominent comprehensive tobacco control initiatives have been enacted, the Master Settlement Agreement (MSA) in the USA in 1998 and the Framework Convention on Tobacco Control (FCTC) at the global level. While there is some formal research, especially on the MSA, the effectiveness of these policies is not yet clear. The MSA between states and tobacco companies was significant in both its scope and magnitude. However, formal investigations of the impacts of this deal are relatively few. Using cross-sectional pooled state-level data, Goel and Nelson's (2006b) paper examines the impact of the MSA on cigarette tax policy at the state level in a political-economy context. From a policy perspective, the evidence suggests that states following 1998 have continued to keep smoking control as a policy objective. That is, MSA payments are viewed as complementary to excise tax increases. More broadly, both economic and political forces seem to exert crucial influences on state tax policy in the post-MSA era. Whether similar consequences will follow on an international scale after the FCTC becomes fully implemented by signatory nations remains to be seen.

Appendix

Table 9A1 MSA settlement payments received by US states (US$ million)

State	2000	2001	2002	2003	2004
Alabama	131.7	96.9	118.6	109.2	99.2
Alaska	27.9	21.2	24.3	23.1	20.9
Arizona	120.3	87.7	107.0	99.6	90.4
Arkansas	69.4	51.3	58.8	55.9	50.8
California	1,031.0	759.2	927.0	862.6	783.2
Colorado	112.2	85.0	97.4	92.6	84.1
Connecticut	150.0	110.4	134.8	125.5	113.9
Delaware	32.0	23.5	28.7	26.7	24.3
DC	34.7	38.0	44.6	44.3	37.3
Florida	674.4	731.3	591.3	546.5	357.3
Georgia	200.8	152.2	174.3	165.8	150.6
Hawaii	48.6	35.8	43.7	40.7	36.9
Idaho	29.7	22.5	26.0	24.5	22.3
Illinois	381.0	288.7	330.6	314.5	285.6
Indiana	167.0	106.5	145.0	137.8	125.2
Iowa	71.2	53.9	61.8	58.7	53.4
Kansas	68.3	51.7	59.2	56.3	51.2
Kentucky	142.2	105.0	127.9	119.0	108.1
Louisiana	184.6	140.0	160.2	152.4	138.4
Maine	63.0	47.3	54.6	52.0	47.2
Maryland	185.0	140.2	160.6	153.0	138.7
Massachusetts	326.2	240.2	293.3	273.0	247.8
Michigan	351.5	258.9	316.0	294.1	267.1
Minnesota	785.5	337.0	368.6	152.9	168.5
Mississippi	479.4	211.2	209.0	149.6	110.3
Missouri	190.7	142.1	161.6	153.7	139.6
Montana	34.7	26.2	30.2	28.7	26.1
Nebraska	48.7	37.0	42.3	40.2	36.5
Nevada	49.9	37.8	43.3	41.2	37.4
New Hampshire	54.5	43.3	47.3	45.0	40.9
New Jersey	318.0	240.0	274.6	261.3	237.3
New Mexico	48.8	37.0	42.3	40.3	36.6
New York	1,030.9	754.3	926.8	862.5	783.1
North Carolina	188.4	142.7	169.4	157.6	143.1
North Dakota	30.0	22.7	26.0	24.7	22.5
Ohio	412.3	312.4	357.8	340.4	309.1
Oklahoma	84.8	64.3	73.6	70.0	63.6
Oregon	92.7	68.3	83.3	77.6	70.4
Pennsylvania	322.3	341.8	417.3	388.4	352.6
Rhode Island	59.0	44.6	51.1	48.6	44.1
South Carolina	96.3	73.0	83.6	79.5	72.2
South Dakota	28.6	21.6	24.8	23.6	21.4

Tennessee	203.0	151.4	173.3	165.0	149.8
Texas	2,236.7	974.2	1,002.8	500.0	479.9
Utah	36.4	27.6	31.6	30.0	27.3
Vermont	33.2	24.5	29.8	27.8	25.2
Virginia	167.3	126.8	145.2	138.2	125.5
Washington	168.0	127.4	145.8	138.8	126.0
West Virginia	72.5	55.0	63.0	60.0	54.4
Wisconsin	167.4	123.2	150.5	140.0	127.1
Wyoming	20.1	14.8	18.0	16.8	15.2
Total	12,062.8	8,229.6	9,278.6	8,030.2	7,179.6

Source: The Tax Burden on Tobacco.

Table 9B1 Signatory nations to FCTC

Country	*Signature year*
Afghanistan	2004
Albania	2004
Algeria	2003
Angola	2004
Antigua and Barbuda	2004
Argentina	2003
Armenia	2004*
Australia	2003
Austria	2003
Azerbaijan	2005*
Bahamas	2004
Bangladesh	2003
Barbados	2004
Belarus	2004
Belgium	2004
Belize	2003
Benin	2004
Bhutan	2003
Bolivia	2004
Botswana	2003
Brazil	2003
Brunei Darussalam	2004
Bulgaria	2003
Burkina Faso	2003
Burundi	2003
Cambodia	2004
Cameroon	2004
Canada	2003

Cape Verde	2004
Central African Republic	2003
Chad	2004
Chile	2003
China	2003
Comoros	2004
Congo	2004
Cook Islands	2004
Costa Rica	2003
Côte d'Ivoire	2003
Croatia	2004
Cuba	2004
Cyprus	2004
Czech Republic	2003
Democratic People's Republic of Korea	2003
Democratic Republic of the Congo	2004
Denmark	2003
Djibouti	2004
Dominica	2004
Ecuador	2004
Egypt	2003
El Salvador	2004
Equatorial Guinea	2005*
Estonia	2004
Ethiopia	2004
European Community	2003
Fiji	2003
Finland	2003
France	2003
Gabon	2003
Gambia	2003
Georgia	2004
Germany	2003
Ghana	2003
Greece	2003
Grenada	2004
Guatemala	2003
Guinea	2004
Guyana	2005*
Haiti	2003
Honduras	2004
Hungary	2003
Iceland	2003
India	2003
Iran	2003
Iraq	2004

Ireland	2003
Israel	2003
Italy	2003
Jamaica	2003
Japan	2004
Jordan	2004
Kazakhstan	2004
Kenya	2004
Kiribati	2004
Kuwait	2003
Kyrgyzstan	2004
Laos People's Democratic Republic	2004
Latvia	2004
Lebanon	2004
Lesotho	2004
Liberia	2004
Libyan Arab Jamahiriya	2004
Lithuania	2003
Luxembourg	2003
Madagascar	2003
Malaysia	2003
Maldives	2004
Mali	2003
Malta	2003
Marshall Islands	2003
Mauritania	2004
Mauritius	2003
Mexico	2003
Micronesia, Federal States of	2004
Mongolia	2003
Morocco	2004
Mozambique	2003
Myanmar	2003
Namibia	2004
Nauru	2004*
Nepal	2003
Netherlands	2003
New Zealand	2003
Nicaragua	2004
Niger	2004
Nigeria	2004
Niue	2004
Norway	2003
Oman	2005*
Pakistan	2004
Palau	2003

Panama	2003
Papua New Guinea	2004
Paraguay	2003
Peru	2004
Philippines	2003
Poland	2004
Portugal	2004
Qatar	2003
Republic of Korea	2003
Republic of Moldova	2004
Romania	2004
Rwanda	2004
Saint Kitts and Nevis	2004
Saint Lucia	2004
Saint Vincent and The Grenadines	2004
Samoa	2003
San Marino	2003
São Tomé and Príncipe	2004
Saudi Arabia	2004
Senegal	2003
Serbia and Montenegro	2004
Seychelles	2003
Singapore	2003
Slovakia	2003
Slovenia	2003
Solomon Islands	2004
South Africa	2003
Spain	2003
Sri Lanka	2003
Sudan	2004
Suriname	2004
Swaziland	2004
Sweden	2003
Switzerland	2004
Syrian Arab Republic	2003
Thailand	2003
The Former Yugoslav Republic of Macedonia	2006*
Timor-Leste	2004
Togo	2004
Tonga	2003
Trinidad and Tobago	2003
Tunisia	2003
Turkey	2004
Tuvalu	2004
Uganda	2004
Ukraine	2004

United Arab Emirates	2004
United Kingdom of Great Britain and Northern Ireland	2003
United Republic of Tanzania	2004
USA	2004
Uruguay	2003
Vanuatu	2004
Venezuela (the Bolivarian Republic of)	2003
Vietnam	2003
Yemen	2003

Source: www.who.int/tobacco/framework/countrylist/en/print.html
*Ratification, acceptance, approval, formal confirmation, accession after June 2004.

Chapter 10

Policy Issues and Directions for Future Research

Tobacco is the second major cause of death in the world. Despite this, nearly half of all adult males and over 10 percent of females are current smokers. Yet, such statistics do not tell the whole story as the composition of tobacco consumers has been changing dramatically over time, calling for new approaches and ideas (see, for example, the research priorities identified in Baris et al. 2000; also see Jha et al. 2006). Tobacco consumption in developed nations seems to have passed the peak and is now slowly declining. In contrast, most developing countries are still experiencing increases in tobacco consumption and today smokers in these countries constitute 70 percent of the global market. Viewed from a different perspective, in the early 1970s consumption was highest in Canada, Switzerland, Australia and the United Kingdom. By the end of the century it was highest in Poland, Greece, Hungary, Japan and the Republic of Korea (World Health Organization, 1996).

Tobacco consumption also varies in important ways across socio-economic groups, including income, age, gender, religion, and educational attainment, as documented in Chapter 1. Gender is especially noteworthy in this regard. For example, smoking prevalence among women actually increases by development level, in direct contrast with men. Further, the teenage smoking prevalence for female teenagers exceeds that of adult women in all regions of the globe with the exception of South-East Asia.

According to the influential report by the Centers for Disease Control, "Current regulation of the advertising and promotion of tobacco products in this country (USA) is considerably less restrictive than in several other countries, notably Canada and New Zealand", (U.S. Department of Health and Human Services, 2000: 18). Our survey in this book shows that nations across the world have been actively trying to combat smoking through various policy measures and the effectiveness of these measures has been the subject of active economics research.

Price (Tax) Tobacco Control Strategies

The price or tax tobacco control initiatives discussed in this book appear to be an effective strategy to reduce smoking, especially for the youth (Chapters 2 and 3). Price elasticity of demand estimates for cigarettes for a large number of studies reviewed by the authors center around -0.4 for adults and around -0.6 for youth. These estimates are somewhat sensitive to the time period used, the data employed and the estimation methodology. For instance, the low cigarette demand elasticity found in many studies of cigarettes seems to have become somewhat more elastic in recent years (see Gallet and List (2003); also Goel and Ram (2004) and Goel and Nelson (2006)). This implies that while the tax revenue generating capabilities might be somewhat undermined with a more elastic demand, there were greater opportunities for inducing smoking reduction.

In formulating public policy on tobacco control it is important to recognize that policy actions directed at one category of tobacco products may have indirect effects on other categories. Cigarettes and smokeless tobacco are obvious examples. If higher excise taxes levied on cigarettes leads to increased consumption of smokeless tobacco then the net health benefits of the higher cigarette taxes will be reduced. Economists measure cross-price relationships between two products with the concept of cross-price elasticity of demand. Earlier evidence calculated the cross-price elasticity for cigarettes and smokeless tobacco to be around 0.4, suggesting that these two products are viewed by consumers as substitutes. However, more recent evidence for the U.S. states summarized in Chapter 3 could not confirm this relationship. The evidence presented in this book suggests that cigarettes and smokeless tobacco are neither substitutes nor complements. It is clear more research is needed in this area. If these two tobacco products are indeed substitutes then it will be important to coordinate tax policy on cigarettes and smokeless tobacco if overall tobacco consumption is to be effectively controlled.[1]

Cross-border smuggling undermines efforts to control smoking as discussed in Chapter 4. It also makes it more difficult for researchers to estimate the responsiveness of cigarette demand to price changes. The relatively long shelf life of tobacco and the tax differentials across various jurisdictions provide incentives for illegal trade. A substantial literature has emerged on cigarette smuggling in the USA and recent evidence suggests that cross-border cigarette sales (both legal and illegal) constitute as much as 13 percent of total market share by the end of the last century. It is also clear that the overall significance of cross-border smuggling is directly related to the cigarette tax differentials among the states/countries.

Tobacco smuggling is also an important phenomenon internationally. Recent estimates of the market share of contraband cigarettes are in the range of six to 10 percent with considerable variation among individual countries. Canada offers a noteworthy example of how international cigarette tax differentials can influence the magnitude of smuggling activity. In the mid-nineties, Canadian tax rates stood at five times the U.S. average and it was estimated the cigarettes smuggled from the U.S. constituted a 30 percent share of the Canadian market (Canadian Cancer Society et al., 1999). More generally, evidence presented in Chapter 4 indicated that overall smuggling activity is indirectly related to a country's stage of development. Finally, the recent proliferation of Internet sales of cigarettes adds an important new dimension to the problem of controlling smuggling activity. At the time of this writing the legal issues regarding governmental jurisdiction to tax Internet sales have not been clarified.

1 Cigarettes and alcohol are two other products that might have interdependencies in demand.

From a policy angle, while tougher laws and monitoring can check organized smuggling, it is less clear what can be done to control casual smuggling (for example tourists buying cheaper tobacco products in other jurisdictions).

Non-price Tobacco Control Strategies

Various non-price measures, such as advertising bans, health warnings and territorial restrictions, were examined in the study. These measures affect the nature of information with smokers and with potential smokers and influence the indirect costs of smoking. Chapter 5 focused on the impact of advertising and advertising bans on cigarette consumption. In general, the econometric studies that have investigated the effect of advertising and other promotional campaigns by tobacco companies have concluded that these initiatives have had only modest positive effects on consumption (Jha et al., 2006). Instead, these efforts seem more effective at redistributing market share among the tobacco companies. The evidence on the impact of advertising restrictions on tobacco companies, such as the 1971 broadcast advertising ban on cigarettes in the U.S., has been mixed. At least some of the reason for the mixed results can be attributed to the nature of the data set used in the analyses (for example level of data aggregation) and econometric techniques used to estimate the various models.

Health warnings, including mandated labels on cigarette packaging and the distribution of other health education materials, were examined in Chapter 6. The U.S. was a leader in mandating warning labels on cigarette packaging with the Federal Cigarette Labeling and Advertising Act of 1965. Since that time other countries such as Australia, Singapore, and Thailand have been at the forefront of enacting even more restrictive requirements in this area. Several econometric investigations into the effectiveness of health warnings have been conducted. While early studies dating back to the mid-eighties concluded that health warnings had little impact on cigarette demand, more recent studies, both for the U.S. and internationally, have concluded that they have been effective in reducing smoking. A problem confronted by researchers in this area is in how to model the qualitative differences among various health warnings (for example warnings on cigarette packages versus point-of-sale (in-store) warnings) and related institutional details.

Another strategy to control smoking is territorial restrictions on where these products can be consumed (for example restrictions in the workplaces and other public places). Also included here are age restrictions on the sale of cigarettes to minors and other policies that restrict their access to these products. Geographic smoking restrictions increase the indirect costs of smoking by making smoking more inconvenient. These policies were discussed further in Chapter 7 along with an assessment of the effectiveness of these strategies.

The extant literature reveals that territorial restrictions have been effective in reducing smoking in the U.S. and in other developed nations where studies have been conducted. Territorial restrictions are relatively rare in developing nations and where they exist they have not been assessed as to their effectiveness. There is also very little in the literature on how effective territorial restrictions are in controlling tobacco consumption among important population subgroups such as the youth.

The economics of smoking cessation was discussed in Chapter 8. In recent decades a variety of approaches have emerged to help people stop smoking in a variety of ways, including nicotine replacement therapies, "quit" telephone help lines, education, and subsidies and rewards for quitting smoking. Private firms have been increasingly involved in promoting and subsidizing smoking cessation programs for their employees as a strategy to fight escalating health care costs.

Analysis of the effectiveness of smoking cessation strategies is only just now emerging at the time of this writing. The early evidence does point to Nicotine Replacement Therapies (NRT) as an effective means to help smokers quit, especially when it was part of a more comprehensive treatment plan and higher cigarette prices. The prices of NRT products do vary substantially across countries and recent consumer studies indicate that the demand for these products is relatively price sensitive.

Over time researchers and policymakers have begun to recognize that effective tobacco control requires the adoption of a comprehensive set of price and non-price policies that are informed by 1) an understanding of the complex set of socio-economic factors that enter into how people make tobacco consumption decisions, and, 2) a recognition of the addictive nature of these products. Comprehensive tobacco control policies, both in the U.S. and internationally are discussed in Chapter 9.

In the U.S. several states have been at the forefront of comprehensive tobacco control programs that date back to the 1980s. The experience of two states – California and Massachusetts – have formed the basis for a set of "best practices" guidelines for comprehensive tobacco control recommended by the Center for Disease Control. State spending on comprehensive tax control varies considerably among the 50 U.S. states and econometric evidence presented in Chapter 9 suggests that states that spend more for this on a per capita basis tend do better in terms of reducing smoking prevalence among the youth. The landmark 1998 Master Settlement Agreement provided for funding for comprehensive tobacco control initiatives at the federal level and provided the resources for states to do more at the local level. At the time of writing, the long-term effects of this agreement on tobacco consumption were still unfolding and awaiting documentation.

Internationally, comprehensive tobacco control varies widely, with low-income countries not performing as well in the area compared with more developed countries.[2] In 2005, the Framework Convention on Tobacco Control – the world's first international health treaty – was entered into force. Its aim was getting signatory states to agree to impose a comprehensive set of non-price tobacco control measures to combat tobacco usage worldwide. As of this writing 168 countries have signed the agreement and 144 countries have ratified the treaty. It is still unclear if and how quickly the goals of the Treaty will be realized once it comes into force.

---

2 It is possible, however, that information about the nature of smoking control initiatives in developing nations might not be as readily available as in the case of developed nations.

Directions for Future Research

While a consensus has emerged that tax (price) policies are an effective strategy to reduce tobacco consumption, the evidence on the effectiveness of non-price measures is mixed. Non-price policy initiatives directed at reducing smoking seem to work in some cases, while other studies find the effects of the same measures to be insignificant. No one measure appears superior to others, although there is some evidence that workplace restrictions are able to reduce smoking. Part of the ambiguity is due to the difficulty of quantifying the institutional regulatory details.

A more overriding practical problem in determining the effectiveness of any smoking control measure is that these measures are seldom enacted in isolation. Rather, many measures are passed simultaneously, with the result that the effectiveness of any single measure is nearly impossible to determine. Better modeling techniques, especially those that allow for multiple policies under the same framework, are needed. Sensitivity analyses of the findings with comparable analysis will aid in determining the robustness of some of the findings. In addition, whereas the dynamics of price elasticities (i.e. short run versus long run elasticities) are well understood, we still do not have a good understanding of the short run and long run effects of non-price measures.

Some of the problems of ambiguous results will be taken care of as better data, especially disaggregated data, become available. Micro level data will enable focus on population subgroups, including race, gender, age, ethnicity, educational and religious backgrounds, and allow for other qualitative differences. For instance, we found little evidence on the effectiveness of health warnings directed at youth.

In addition to what we have discussed above, we list below some directions for future research that would enable better understanding of cigarette demand and help policy makers in framing more effective policies to check smoking.

- In thinking about the effectiveness of smoking control policies, one must also keep in mind the two-way causality between the demand and supply of these policies. On the one hand, countries might enact policies to combat high smoking rates; on the other hand, relatively low smoking prevalence in a country might not warrant an aggressive anti-smoking campaign. Stated differently, the lack of comprehensive anti-smoking legislation in a country might be understood in the context of its low smoking rates. For example, countries like the USA do not have very strong anti-smoking policies when compared with countries like Norway, Singapore and Australia. These policies might be unwarranted in light of the relatively low smoking rates in the U.S.
- We need a better understanding of the relation of cigarettes with other products including alcohol and other types of tobacco products (i.e. cross-price elasticities). To what extent are smokers substituting different types of tobacco products? A well-defined cross-price elasticity will have implications for spillovers from the cigarette market to related markets. This is especially significant in cases of nations where some tobacco products are less regulated than cigarettes (for example India and Indonesia).
- Some attention is being devoted in recent years to smoking cessation initiatives

(Chapter 8). Why some smokers experience a relapse after quitting smoking while others do not is still not very well understood. Another interesting line of research in this context concerns the responsiveness of smokers to prices of cessation treatments (see, for example, Chaloupka and Tauras, 2004).

- A caveat about the literature on cigarette demand and advertising is in order. Cigarette advertising data have different components and their availability and aggregation is not consistent over time or across countries. For example, even after the broadcast ban, firms continue to advertise in various forms: print, billboards, promotions, in-store displays, sports promotions, etc. until the 1998 Master Settlement Agreement in case of the USA. It is not clear how qualitatively different these advertising forms are and what, if any, is the difference in their lag structure. Further, cigarette advertising "may simultaneously persuade, inform, and create desirable product images" (Tremblay and Tremblay, 1995). We need a better understanding of the qualitative differences between the various forms of advertising (see Nelson, 2006).
- We found an alarming lack of research focusing on smoking behavior in developing nations where tobacco consumption is relatively high. This is especially relevant since there are a number of unregulated tobacco products, other than cigarettes, in developing countries. For instance, cigarettes form only about 65-85 percent of all tobacco consumption (WHO, 1996).
- The spread of the Internet has added an entirely new dimension to tobacco control. Legal issues regarding the taxation of Internet sales are still in need of clarification and the practicality of taxing these sales can be problematic. All of this reduces the effectiveness to price (tax) strategies to combat tobacco consumption. As to the various non-price tobacco control strategies, advertising can now freely move across national boundaries, creating difficulties for enforcement and regulation. Policy makers will have to rethink the regulation of cigarette advertising, especially when the honeymoon with the Internet ends.

In closing, this book has tried to examine the effectiveness of smoking control initiatives around the world. The interest in tobacco control has heightened in recent years among the various constituencies – lawmakers, researchers and the public. Given the nexus of various disciplines in terms of their bearing on tobacco use (for example economics, marketing, psychology, medicine, etc.), greater research collaboration among various fields is warranted. Overall, while significant strides have been made in checking tobacco use, especially among adults in developed nations, policymakers have their work cut out investigating whether and how the smoking control policies will work in other instances such as youth and developing nations. Until then, a "smoke-free" planet will sadly remain a pipe dream.

Bibliography

Advisory Commission on Intergovernmental Relations (ACIR) (1977), *Cigarette Bootlegging: A State and Federal Responsibility* (Washington, DC: Advisory Commission on Intergovernmental Relations).

Advisory Commission on Intergovernmental Relations (ACIR) (1985), *Cigarette Tax Evasion: A Second Look* (Washington, DC: Advisory Commission on Intergovernmental Relations).

Aftab, M., Kolben, D., Lurie, P. and Wolfe, S. (1998), *Smokescreen: Double Standards of U.S. Tobacco Companies in International Cigarette Labeling* (Washington, DC: Public Citizen's Health Research Group).

Alciati, M.H., Frosh, M., Green, S.B., Brownson, R.C., Fisher, P.H., Hobart, R., Roman, A., Sciandra, R.C. and Shelton, D.M. (1998), "State Laws on Youth Access to Tobacco in the United States: Measuring their Extensiveness with a New Rating System", *Tobacco Control*, 7, 345–352. [PubMed 10093166]

American Cancer Society, Inc. (2003), World Health Organization and International Union Against Cancer, *Tobacco Control Country Profiles*, (2nd edition), Atlanta, GA., http://www.globalink.org/tccp/.

Atkinson, A.B. and Skeggs, J.L. (1973), "Anti-Smoking Publicity and the Demand for Tobacco in the U.K.," *Manchester School of Economic and Social Studies*. **41**, (3), 265–282.

Baltagi, B.H. and Goel, R.K. (1987), "Quasi-Experimental Price Elasticities of Cigarette Demand and the Bootlegging Effect", *American Journal of Agricultural Economics*, **69**(4), 750–754. [DOI: 10.2307/1242184].

Baltagi, B.H. and Goel, R.K. (1990), "Quasi-Experimental Price Elasticity of Liquor Demand in the United States: 1960–83", *American Journal of Agricultural Economics*, **72**(2), 451–454. [DOI: 10.2307/1242348].

Baltagi, B.H. and Goel, R.K. (2004), "State Tax Changes and Quasi-Experimental Price Elasticities of U.S. Cigarette Demand: An Update", *Journal of Economics and Finance*, **28**, 422–429.

Baltagi, B.H. and Levin, D. (1986), "Estimating Dynamic Demand for Cigarettes Using Panel Data: The Effects of Bootlegging, Taxation and Advertising Reconsidered". *Review of Economics and Statistics*, **68**(1), 148–155. [DOI: 10.2307/1924938].

Baltagi, B.H. and Levin, D. (1992), "Cigarette Taxation: Raising Revenues and Reducing Consumption", *Structural Change and Economic Dynamics*, **3**(2), 321–335. [DOI: 10.1016/0954–349X%2892%2990010–4].

Bardsley, P. and Olekalns, N. (1999), "Cigarette and Tobacco Consumption: Have Anti-Smoking Policies Made a Difference?" *Economic Record*, **75**, 225–240.

Barford, M.F. (1993), "New Dimensions Boost Cigarette Smuggling", *Tobacco Journal International*, **3**, 16–18.

Baris, E., Brigden, L.W., Prindville, J., Salva, V., Chitanonh, H. and Chandiwana, S. (2000), "Research Priorities for Tobacco Control in Developing Countries: A Regional Approach to Global Consultative Process", *Tobacco Control*, **9**, 217–223. [DOI: 10.1136/tc.9.2.217].

BBC News (2001, July 07), "Europe Smuggling Case Up in Smoke". http://news.bbc.co.uk/1/hi/world/europe/1444842.stm.

Becker, G.S. and Murphy, K.M. (1988), "A Theory of Rational Addiction", *Journal of Political Economy*, **96**(4), 675–700. [DOI: 10.1086/261558].

Becker, G.S., Grossman, M. and Murphy, K.M. (1994), "An Empirical Analysis of Cigarette Addiction", *American Economic Review*, **84**(3), 396–418.

Bhagwati, J. and Hansen, B. (1973), "Theoretical Analysis of Smuggling", *The Quarterly Journal of Economics*, **87**(2), 172–187. [DOI: 10.2307/1882182].

Bishop, J.A. and Yoo, J.H. (1985), "Health Scare, Excise Taxes and Advertising Ban in the Cigarette Demand and Supply," *Southern Economic Journal*, **52**(2), 402–411.

Blaine, T.W. and Reed, M.R. (1994), "U.S. Cigarette Smoking and Health Warnings: New Evidence from Post World War II Data", *Journal of Agricultural and Applied Economics*, **26**, 535–544.

Boddewyn, J.J. (1994), "Cigarette Advertising Bans and Smoking: The Flawed Policy Connection", *International Journal of Advertising*, **13**, 311–332.

Borland, R. (1997), "Tobacco Health Warning and Smoking-Related Cognitions and Behaviours", *Addiction*, **92**(11), 1427–1436. [PubMed 9519486] [DOI: 10.1111/j.1360–0443.1997.tb02864.x].

Borland, R. and Hill, D. (1997), "Initial Impact of the New Australian Tobacco Health Warnings on Knowledge and Beliefs", *Tobacco Control*, **6**, 317–325. [PubMed 9583630].

Borland, R., Owen, N. and Hocking, B. (1991), "Changes in Smoking Behaviour after a Total Workplace Smoking Ban", *Australian Journal of Public Health*, **15**(2), 130–134. [PubMed 1912055].

Brenner, H. and Mielck, A. (1992), "Smoking Prohibition in the Workplace and Smoking Cessation in the Federal Republic of Germany", *Preventive Medicine*, **21**(2), 252–261. [PubMed 1579559] [DOI: 10.1016/0091–7435%2892%2990023–B].

Bulow, J. (2003), "Review Article: Profiting from Smokers", *Southern Economic Journal*, **69**, 736–742. [DOI: 10.2307/1061706]

Bulow, J.I. and Klemperer, P.D. (1998), "The Tobacco Deal," *Brookings Papers on Economic Activity – Microeconomics*, 323–394.

Calfee, J.E. and Scheraga, C.A. (1994), "The Influence of Advertising on Alcohol Consumption: A Literature Review and an Econometric Analysis of Four European Nations", *International Journal of Advertising*, **13**, 287–310.

Cameron, S. (1997), "Are Greek Smokers Rational Addicts?" *Applied Economics Letters*, **4**, 401–402. [DOI: 10.1080/135048597355122].

Cameron, S. (1998), "Estimation of the Demand for Cigarettes: A Review of The Literature", *Economic Issues*, **3**, 51–71.

Campaign for Tobacco-Free Kids (2005, October 21) *Internet Tobacco Sales* http://www.tobaccofreekids.org/reports/internet/.

Canadian Cancer Society (2002), *Evaluation of New Warnings on Cigarette Packages,* Ottawa.

Canadian Cancer Society, Non-Smokers, Rights Association, Physicians for a Smoke-Free Canada, Quebec Coalition for Tobacco Control. (1999). *Surveying the Damage: Cut-Rate Tobacco Products and Public Health in the 1990s.* Ottawa.

Capehart, T. (2004), *Trends in U.S. Tobacco Farming,* (U.S. Department of Agriculture), TBS–257–02, November.

Capehart, T.C., Jr (2001), *Trends in the Cigarette Industry after the Master Settlement Agreement,* (U.S. Department of Agriculture), TBS–250–01, www.ers.usda.gov.

Centers for Disease Control and Prevention (CDC) (1999), *Best Practices for Tobacco Control Programs – August 1999.* Atlanta GA: U.S. Department of Health and Human Services, Center for Disease Control and Prevention, National Center for Chronic Disease Prevention and Health Promotion, Office of Smoking and Health.

Centers for Disease Control and Prevention (CDC) (2000), *Reducing Tobacco Use: A Report of the Surgeon General* (Atlanta, GA: U.S. Department of Health and Human Services, Centers for Disease Control and Prevention, Office on Smoking and Health.

Centers for Disease Control and Prevention (CDC) (2004), "Sustaining Programs for Tobacco Control, Data Highlights". www.cdc.gov/tobacco/datahighlights/.

Centers for Disease Control and Prevention (CDC), *Percentage of Adults who were Current, Former, or Never Smokers, Overall and by Sex, Race, Hispanic Origin, Age, and Education* National Health Interview Surveys, Selected Years – USA, 1965–2000, www.cdc.gov/tobacco/research_data/adults_prev/adstat1.htm.

Centers for Disease Control and Prevention (CDC), *State Tobacco Activities Tracking and Evaluation (STATE) System*, http://www.cdc.gov/tobacco/statesystem.

Chaloupka, F.J. (1991), "Rational Addictive Behavior and Cigarette Smoking", *Journal of Political Economy*, **99**, 722–742. [DOI: 10.1086/261776].

Chaloupka, F.J. (1995), "Public Policies and Private Anti-Health Behavior", *American Economic Review Papers and Proceedings*, **85**(2), 45–49.

Chaloupka, F.J. and Saffer, H. (1988). *The Demand for Cigarettes and Restrictions on Smoking in the Workplace* (NBER Working Paper 2663).

Chaloupka, F.J. and Tauras, J.A. (2004), "The Impact of Nicotine Replacement Therapies on Cigarette Demand", *Journal of Economics and Finance*, **28**, 395–403.

Chaloupka, F.J. and Wakefield, M. (2000), "Effectiveness of Comprehensive Tobacco Control Programmes in Reducing Teenage Smoking in the USA", *Tobacco Control*, **9**, 177–186. [PubMed 10841854] [DOI: 10.1136/tc.9.2.177].

Chaloupka, F.J. and Warner, K.E. (2000), "The Economics of Smoking" in *Handbook of Health Economics*, Culyer, A.J. and Newhouse, J.P. (eds.) (Amsterdam: North-Holland), 1539–1627.

Chaloupka, F.J. and Wechsler, H. (1995). *Price, Tobacco Control Policies and Smoking Control among Young Adults*. (NBER Working Paper W5012).

Chapman, S. and Carter, S.M. (2003), "Avoid Health Warnings on All Tobacco Products For Just As Long As We Can: A History of Australian Tobacco Industry Efforts to Avoid, Delay and Dilute Health Warnings on Cigarettes", *Tobacco Control*, **12**, 13–22. [DOI: 10.1136/tc.12.2.113].

Chapman, S. and Richardson, J. (1990), "Tobacco Excise and Declining Tobacco Consumption: The Case of Papua New Guinea", *American Journal of Public Health*, **80**(5), 537–540. [PubMed 2327528].

Chetwynd, J., Coope, P., Brodie, R.J. and Wells, E. (1988), "Impact of Cigarette Advertising on Aggregate Demand for Cigarettes in New Zealand", *Addiction*, **83**(4), 409–414. [DOI: 10.1111/j.1360–0443.1988.tb00487.x].

Clements, K.W., McLeod, P.B. and Selvanathan, E.A. (1985), "Does Advertising Affect Drinking and Smoking?", mimeo, University of Western Australia.

Coates, R.M. (1995), "A Note on Estimating Cross-Border Effects of State Cigarette Taxes", *National Tax Journal*, **48**(4), 573–584.

Cohen, J.E., Sarabia, V. and Ashley, M.J. (2001), "Tobacco Commerce on the Internet: A Threat to Comprehensive Tobacco Control", *Tobacco Control*, **10**, 364–367. [PubMed 11740029] [DOI: 10.1136/tc.10.4.364].

Conniffe, D. (1995), "Models of Irish Tobacco Consumption", *Economic and Social Review*, **26**(4), 331–347.

Cox, H. and Smith, R. (1984), "Political Approaches to Smoking Control: A Comparative Analysis", *Applied Economics*, **16**(4), 569–582.

Cutler, D.M., Gruber, J., Hartman, R.S., Landrum, M.B. and Newhouse, J.P., & Rosenthal, M. B (2002), "The Economic Impacts of the Tobacco Settlement," *Journal of Policy Analysis and Management*, **21**, 1–19.

Czart, C., Pacula, R.L., Chaloupka, F.J. and Wechsler, H. (2001), "The Impact of Prices and Control Policies on Cigarette Smoking among College Students", *Contemporary Economic Policy*, **19**(2), 135–149. [DOI: 10.1093/cep%2F19.2.135].

DeCicca, P., Kenkel, D. and Mathios, A. (2002), "Putting Out the Fires: Will Higher Taxes Reduce the Onset of Youth Smoking?" *Journal of Political Economy*, **110**(1), 144–169. [DOI: 10.1086/324386].

Dee, S.T. (1999), "The Complementarity of Teen Smoking and Drinking", *Journal of Health Economics*, **18**, 769–793. [PubMed 10847934] [DOI: 10.1016/S0167–6296%2899%2900018–1].

Doroodian, K. and Seldon, B.J. (1991), "Advertising and Cigarette Consumption," *Eastern Economic Journal*, **17**, 359–366.

Douglas, S. (1998), "The Duration of the Smoking Habit", *Economic Inquiry*, **36**(1), 49–64.

Duffy, M. (1996a), "Econometric Studies of Advertising, Advertising Restrictions and Cigarette Demand: A Survey", *International Journal of Advertising*, **15**, 1–23.

Duffy, M. (1996b), "An Econometric Study of Advertising and Cigarette Demand in the United Kingdom", *International Journal of Advertising*, **15**, 262–284.

Eckard, E.W. (1991), "Competition and the Cigarette TV Advertising Ban", *Economic Inquiry*, **29**(1), 119–133.

Evans, W.N. and Ringel, J.S. (1999), "Can Higher Cigarette Taxes Improve Birth Outcomes?" *Journal of Public Economics*, **72**, 135–154. [DOI: 10.1016/S0047–2727%2898%2900090–5].

Farrelly, M.C., Bray, J.W., Pechacek, T. and Woollery, T. (2001), "Response by Adults to Increase in Cigarette Prices by Sociodemographic Characteristics", *Southern Economic Journal*, **68**(1), 156–165. [DOI: 10.2307/1061518].

Farrelly, M.C., Pechacek, T.F. and Chaloupka, F.J. (2003), "The Impact of Tobacco Control Program Expenditure on Aggregate Tobacco Sales: 1981–2000", *Journal of Health Economics*, **23**(2), 843–859. [DOI: 10.1016/S0167–6296%2803%2900057–2].

Federation of Tax Administrators, *State Excise Tax Rates on Cigarettes*, http://www.taxadmin.org/fta/rate/cigarette.html.

Fichtenberg, C.M. and Glantz, S.A. (2002), "Effect of Smoke-Free Workplaces on Smoking Behaviour: Systematic Review", *British Medical Journal*, **325**, 188–191. [PubMed 12142305] [DOI: 10.1136/bmj.325.7357.188].

Flay, B.R. (1987), "Mass Media and Smoking Cessation: A Critical Review", *American Journal of Public Health*, **77**(2), 153–160. [PubMed 3541650].

Fleenor, P.W. (1998). *How Excise Tax Differentials Affect Interstate Smuggling and Cross-Border Sales of Cigarettes in the United States*, Background Paper No. 26. Tax Foundation.

Food and Agriculture Organization, of the United Nations (FAO) (2003)*Projections of Tobacco Production, Consumption and Trade to the Year 2010*. http://www.fao.org/DOCREP/006/Y4956E/y4956e04.htm#bm04.1.2.

Fowler, S.J. and Ford, W.F. (2004), "Has a Quarter-Trillion Dollar Settlement Helped the Tobacco Industry?" *Journal of Economics and Finance*, **28**, 430–444.

Fox, W.F. (1986), "Tax Structure and the Location of Economic Activity along State Borders", *National Tax Journal*, **39**, 387–401.

Gajalakshmi C.K., Jha P., Ranson K. and Nguyen S. (2000), "Global Patterns of Smoking and Smoking-Attributable Mortality", in *Tobacco Control in Developing Countries*, Jha, P. and Chaloupka, F. (eds.) (Oxford: Oxford University Press), 11–39.

Galbraith, J.W. and Kaiserman, M. (1997), "Taxation, Smuggling and Demand for Cigarettes in Canada: Evidence from Time-Series Data", *Journal of Health Economics*, **16**(3), 287–301. [PubMed 10169302] [DOI: 10.1016/S0167–6296%2896%2900525–5].

Gallet, C. and Agarwal, R. (1999), "The Gradual Response of Cigarette Demand to Health Information", *Bulletin of Economic Research*, **51**, 259-265.

Gallet, C.A. and List, J.A. (2003), "Cigarette Demand: A Meta-Analysis of Elasticities", *Health Economics*, **12**, 821–835.

General Accounting Office (GAO) (2002), *Internet Cigarette Sales: Giving ATF Investigative Authority May Improve Reporting and Enforcement*, GAO–02–GAO743 (District of Columbia: Washington): USGPO.

Glied, S. (2002), "Youth Tobacco Control: Reconciling Theory and Empirical Evidence", *Journal of Health Economics*, **21**(1), 117–135. [PubMed 11845920] [DOI: 10.1016/S0167–6296%2801%2900118–7].

Goel, R.K. (1994), "Quasi-Experimental Taxation Elasticities of U.S. Gasoline Demand", *Energy Economics*, **16**(2), 133–137. [DOI: 10.1016/0140–9883%2894%2990007–8].

Goel, R.K. (2004), "Cigarette Demand in Canada and U.S.-Canadian Cigarette Smuggling", *Applied Economics Letters*, **11**, 537–540. [DOI: 10.1080/1350485042000263043].

Goel, R.K. (forthcoming), "Costs of Smoking and Attempts to Quit", *Applied Economics*.

Goel, R.K. and Morey, M.J. (1995), "The Interdependence of Cigarette and Liquor Demand", *Southern Economic Journal*, **62**, 451–459. [DOI: 10.2307/1060696].

Goel, R.K., and Nelson, M.A. (2004), "International Patterns of Cigarette Smoking and Global Anti-Smoking Policies", *Journal of Economics and Finance*, **28**, 382–394.

Goel, R.K. and Nelson, M.A. (2005), "Tobacco Policy and Tobacco Use: Differences across Tobacco Types, Gender and Age", *Applied Economics*, **37**, 765–771.

Goel, R.K., and Nelson, M.A. (2006), "The Effectiveness of Anti-Smoking Legislation: A Review", *Journal of Economic Surveys*, **20**, 325–356.

Goel, R.K., and Nelson, M.A. (2006b). *The Master Settlement Agreement and Cigarette Tax Policy*, mimeo, Illinois State University.

Grossman, M. (1989), "Health Benefits of Increases in Alcohol and Cigarette Taxes", *Addiction*, **84**(10), 1193–1204. [DOI: 10.1111/j.1360–0443.1989.tb00715.x].

Grossman, M., Sindelar, J. L., Mullahy, J. and Anderson, R. (1993), "Policy Watch: Alcohol and Cigarette Taxes", *Journal of Economic Perspectives*, **7**(4), 211–222.

Gruber, J. (2001), "Tobacco at the Crossroads: The Past and Future of Smoking Regulation in the United States", *Journal of Economic Perspectives*, **15**(2), 193–212.

Gruber, J. and Koszegi, B. (2001), "Is Addiction "Rational"? Theory and Evidence", *Quarterly Journal of Economics*, **116**, 1261–1303. [DOI: 10.1162/003355301753265570].

Gruber, J., Sen, A. and Stabile, M. (2003), "Estimating Price Elasticities when there is Smuggling: The Sensitivity of Smoking to Price in Canada", *Journal of Health Economics*, **22**, 821–842.

Guindon, G.E., Tobin, S. and Yach, D. (2002), "Trends and Affordability of Cigarette Prices: Ample Room for Tax Increases and Related Health Gains", *Tobacco Control*, **11**, 35–43. [PubMed 11891366] [DOI: 10.1136/tc.11.1.35].

Hamilton, J.L. (1972), "The Demand for Cigarettes: Advertising, the Health Scare, and the Advertising Ban", *Review of Economics and Statistics*, **54**(4), 401–411. [DOI: 10.2307/1924567].

Hammond, D., Fong, G.T., McDonald, P.W., Cameron, R. and Brown, K.S. (2003), "Impact of the Graphic Canadian Warning Labels on Adult Smoking Behavior", *Tobacco Control*, **12**, 391–395. [DOI: 10.1136/tc.12.4.391].

Harris, W.T. and Harris, L. (1996), "The Decision to Quit Smoking: Theory and Evidence", *Journal of Socio-Economics*, **25**, 601–618. [DOI: 10.1016/S1053–5357%2896%2990020–7].

Health Canada *New Cigarette Labeling Measures*. www.hc-sc.gc.ca.

Hettich, W. and Winer, S.L. (1988), "Economic and Political Foundations of Tax Structure", *American Economic Review*, **78**, 701–712.

Hettich, W. and Winer, S.L. (1998), *Democratic Choice and Taxation* (New York: Cambridge University Press).

Hirschberg, J.G., Maasoumi, E., Slottje, D. & Arize, A.C., (2003), "Antitrust Issues in International Comparisons of Market Structure", *Journal of Econometrics*, **113**, 129-158.

Houthakker, H.S. and Taylor, L.D. (1970), *Consumer Demand in the United States 1929–1970: Analyses and Projections* (Cambridge: Harvard University Press).

Hsieh, C.R. (1998), "Health Risk and the Decision to Quit Smoking", *Applied Economics*, **30**(6), 795–804. [DOI: 10.1080/000368498325499].

Hu, T.W., Sung, H.Y. and Keeler, T.E. (1995a), "Reducing Cigarette Consumption in California: Tobacco Taxes vs. An Anti-Smoking Media Campaign", *American Journal of Public Health*, **85**, 1218–1222.

Hu, T.W., Sung, H.Y. and Keeler, T.E. (1995b), "The State Antismoking Campaign and the Industry Response: The Effects of Advertising on Cigarette Consumption in California", *American Economic Review*, **85**(2), 85–90.

Hughes, J.R., Shiffman, S., Callas, P. and Zhang, J. (2003), "A Meta-Analysis of the Efficacy of Over-the-Counter Nicotine Replacement", *Tobacco Control*, **12**, 21–27. [PubMed 12612357] [DOI: 10.1136/tc.12.1.21].

Hunter, W.J. and Nelson, M.A. (1990), "Excise Taxation and the Theory of Tax Exploitation", *Public Finance/Finances Publiques,* **45**, 269–282.

Hunter, W.J. and Nelson, M.A. (1992), "The Political Economy of State Tobacco Taxation", *Public Finance/Finances Publiques*, **47**, 111–125.

Jacobson, P.D. and Wasserman, J. (1997), *Tobacco Control Laws* (Santa Monica, CA: Rand Corporation).

Jha, P. and Chaloupka, F.J. (eds) (2000), *Tobacco Control in Developing Countries* (London: Oxford University Press).

Jha, P., Chaloupka, F.J., Corrao, M. and Jacob, B. (2006), "Reducing the Burden of Smoking World-Wide: Effectiveness of Interventions and their Coverage", *Drug and Alcohol Review*, **25**, 597–609. [PubMed 17132576] [DOI: 10.1080/095952 30600944511].

Jha, P., Ranson, M.K., Nguyen, S.N. and Yach, D. (2002), "Estimates of Global and Regional Smoking Prevalence in 1995, by Age and Sex", *American Journal of Public Health*, **92**(6), 1002–1006. [PubMed 12036796].

Johnson, L.W. (1986), "Advertising Expenditure and Aggregate Demand for Cigarettes in Australia", *International Journal of Advertising*, **5**, 45–58.

Joossens, L., Tobacco Smuggling, Tobacco Control Factsheets. http://factsheets.globalink.org/en/smuggling.shtml.

Joossens, L., Chaloupka, F.J., Merriman, D. and Yuekli, A. (2000), "Issues in the Smuggling of Tobacco Products", in *Tobacco Control in Developing Countries*, Jha, P. and Chaloupka, F. (eds) (Oxford: Oxford University Press), 393–406.

Joossens, L. and Raw, M. (1995), "Smuggling and Cross Border Shopping of Tobacco in Europe", *British Medical Journal*, **310**, 1393–1397. [PubMed 7787549].

Joossens, L. and Raw, M. (1998), "Cigarette Smuggling in Europe: Who Really Benefits?" *Tobacco Control*, **7**, 66–71. [PubMed 9706757].

Keeler, T.E., Hu, T.W., Barnett, P.G. and Manning, W.G. (1993), "Taxation, Regulation, and Addiction: A Demand Function for Cigarettes Based on Time-Series Evidence", *Journal of Health Economics*, **12**(1), 1–18. [PubMed 10126486] [DOI: 10.1016/0167–6296%2893%2990037–F].

Keeler, T.E., Hu, T.W., Barnett, P.G., Manning, W.G. and Sung, H.Y. (1996), "Do Cigarette Producers Price-Discriminate by State? An Empirical Analysis of Local Cigarette Pricing and Taxation", *Journal of Health Economics*, **15**(4), 499–512. [PubMed 10164041] [DOI: 10.1016/S0167–6296%2896%2900498–5].

Keeler, T.E., Hu, T.W., Ong, M. and Sung, H.Y. (2004), "The US National Tobacco Settlement: The Effects of Advertising and Price Changes on Cigarette Consumption", *Applied Economics*, **36**, 1623–1629. [DOI: 10.1080/0003684042 000266829].

Kenkel, D. and Chen, L. (2000), "Consumer Information and Tobacco Use", in *Tobacco Control in Developing Countries*, Jha, P. and Chaloupka, F. (eds.), 177–214.

Kidd, M.P. and Hopkins, S. (2004), "The Hazards of Starting and Quitting Smoking: Some Australian Evidence", *Economic Record*, **80**, 177–192.

Kmenta, J. (1971), *Elements of Econometrics* (New York: Macmillan).

Lamdin, D.J. (1999), "Event Studies of Regulation and New Results on the Effect of the Cigarette Advertising Ban", *Journal of Regulatory Economics*, **16**(2), 187–201. [DOI: 10.1023/A%3A1008197018776].

Lance, P.M., Akin, J.S., Dow, W.H. and Loh, C.P. (2004), "Is Cigarette Smoking in Poorer Nations Highly Sensitive to Price? Evidence from Russia and China", *Journal of Health Economics*, **23**, 173–189. [PubMed 15154693] [DOI: 10.1016/j.jhealeco.2003.09.004].

Lanoie, P. and Leclair, P. (1998), "Taxation or Regulation: Looking for a Good Anti-Smoking Policy", *Economics Letters*, **58**(1), 85–89. [DOI: 10.1016/S0165–1765%2897%2900258–9].

Laugesen, M. and Meads, C. (1991), "Tobacco Advertising Restrictions, Price, Income, and Tobacco Consumption in OECD Countries, 1960–86", *Addiction*, **86**(10), 1343–1354. [DOI: 10.1111/j.1360–0443.1991.tb01710.x].

Laxminarayan, R. and Deolalikar, A. (2004), "Tobacco Initiation, Cessation, and Change: Evidence from Vietnam", *Health Economics*, **13**(12), 1191–1201. [PubMed 15386650] [DOI: 10.1002/hec.932].

Leahy, A.S. (1997), "Advertising and Concentration: A Survey of the Empirical Evidence", *Quarterly Journal of Business and Economics*, **36**, 35–50.

Leu, R.E. (1984), "Anti-Smoking Publicity, Taxation, and the Demand for Cigarettes", *Journal of Health Economics*, **3**(2), 101–116. [PubMed 10268368] [DOI: 10.1016/0167–6296%2884%2990001–8].

Levy, D.E. and Meara, E. (2006), "The Effect of the 1998 Master Settlement Agreement on Prenatal Smoking", *Journal of Health Economics*, **25**, 276–294. [PubMed 16139908] [DOI: 10.1016/j.jhealeco.2005.07.006].

Lewit, E.M., Coate, D. and Grossman, M. (1981), "The Effects of Government Regulation on Teenage Smoking", *Journal of Law and Economics*, **24**(3), 545–569. [DOI: 10.1086/466999].

Lewit, E.M., Hyland, A., Kerrebrock, N. and Cummings, K.M. (1997), "Price, Public Policy, and Smoking in Young People", *Tobacco Control*, **6**, 17–24. [DOI: 10.1136/tc.6.suppl_2.S17].

Lyon, H.L. and Simon, J.L. (1968), "Price Elasticity of the Demand for Cigarettes in the United States", *American Journal of Agricultural Economics*, **50**(4), 888–895. [DOI: 10.2307/1237626].

Mackay, J. and Eriksen, M. (2002), *The Tobacco Atlas*, World Health Organization.

Mahood, G. (1995), "Canadian Tobacco Package Warning System", *Tobacco Control*, **4**, 10–14.

Manchester, P.B. (1976), "Interstate Cigarette Smuggling", *Public Finance Quarterly*, **4**(2), 225–238.

Manning, W.G., Keeler, E.B., Newhouse, J.P., Sloss, E.M. and Wasserman, J. (1989), "The Taxes of Sin. Do Smokers and Drinkers Pay their Way?" *The Journal of the American Medical Association*, **261**(11), 1604–1609. [DOI: 10.1001/jama.261.11.1604].

Marks, L. (1982), "Policies and Postures in Smoking Control", *British Medical Journal*, **284**, 391–395. [PubMed 6800472].

McFadden, D. (1999), "Rationality for Economists?" *Journal of Risk and Uncertainty*, **19**, 1–3, 73–105.

McGowan, R. (1995), *Business, Politics, and Cigarettes: Multiples Levels, Multiple Agendas* (Westport, CT: Quorum Books).

Merriman, D. (2002), "Cigarette Smuggling Does Not Reduce the Public Health Benefit of Cigarette Taxes", *Applied Economics Letters*, **9**(8), 493–496. [DOI: 10.1080/13504850110095468].

Merriman, D., Yurekli, A. and Chaloupka, F.J. (2000), "How Big is the Worldwide Cigarette-Smuggling Problem?" in *Tobacco Control in Developing Countries*, Jha, P. and Chaloupka, F.J. (eds) (London: Oxford University Press), 365–392.

Messinis, G. (1999), "Habit Formation and the Theory of Addiction", *Journal of Economic Surveys*, **13**(4), 417–442. [DOI: 10.1111/1467–6419.00089].

Mitchell, M.L. and Mulherin, J.H. (1988), "Finessing the Political System: The Cigarette Advertising Ban", *Southern Economic Journal*, **54**, 855–862. [DOI: 10.2307/1059521].

Nelson, J.P. (2003), "Cigarette Demand, Structural Change, and Advertising Bans: International Evidence, 1970–1995", *Contributions to Economic Analysis and Policy*, **2**, 1–27.

Nelson, J.P. (2006), "Cigarette Advertising Regulation: A Review", *International Review of Law and Economics*, **26**, 195–226. [DOI: 10.1016/j.irle.2006.08.005].

Nelson, M.A. (2002), "Using Excise Taxes to Finance State Government: Do Neighboring State Taxation Policy and Cross-Border Markets Matter?" *Journal of Regional Science*, **42**, 731–752. [DOI: 10.1111/1467–9787.00279].

Norton, D.A.G. (1988), "On the Economic Theory of Smuggling", *Economica*, **55**, 107–118. [DOI: 10.2307/2554250].

Novotny, T.E., Cohen, J.C., Yurekli, A., Sweanor, D. and Beyer, J.D. (2000), "Smoking Cessation and Nicotine-Replacement Therapies", in *Tobacco Control in Developing Countries*, Jha, P. and Chaloupka, F.J. (eds) (Oxford: Oxford University Press), 287–307, http://www1.worldbank.org/tobacco/tcdc/287TO308.PDF.

Ohsfeldt, R.L. and Boyle, R.G. (1994), "Tobacco Excise Taxes and Rates of Smokeless Tobacco Use in the U.S.: An Exploratory Ecological Analysis", *Tobacco Control*, **3**, 316–323.

Ohsfeldt, R.L. and Boyle, R.G., & Capilouto. E (1997), "Effects of Tobacco Excise Taxes on the Use of Smokeless Tobacco Products in the USA", *Health Economics*, **6**, 525–531.

Orzechowski and Walker (various years). *The Tax Burden on Tobacco: Historical Compilation.* Arlington, VA: Orzechowski and Walker.

Pechmann, C. and Ratneshwar, S. (1994), "The Effects of Antismoking and Cigarette Advertising on Young Adolescents' Perceptions of Peers who Smoke", *Journal of Consumer Research*, **21**, 236–251. [DOI: 10.1086/209395].

Pekurinen, M. (1989), "The Demand for Tobacco Products in Finland", *Addiction*, **84**, 1183–1192. [DOI: 10.1111/j.1360–0443.1989.tb00714.x].

Radfar, M. (1985), "The Effect of Advertising on Total Consumption of Cigarettes in the U.K.", *European Economic Review*, **29**, 225–231. [DOI: 10.1016/0014–2921%2885%2990053–4].

Ramsey, J.B. and Schmidt, P. (1976), "Some Further Results on the Use of OLS and BLUS Residuals in Specification Error Tests", *Journal of the American Statistical Association*, **71**, 389–390. [DOI: 10.2307/2285320].

Ranson, K., Jha, P., Chaloupka, F.J. and Nguyen, S. (2000), "The Effectiveness and Cost-Effectiveness of Price Increases and Other Tobacco-Control Policies", in *Tobacco Control in Developing Countries*, Jha, P. and Chaloupka, F. (eds) (Oxford: Oxford University Press), 427–447.

Roemer, R. (1993), *Legislative Action to Combat the World Tobacco Epidemic*, 2nd edn (Geneva: World Health Organization).

Rogozski, J. (1990), *Smokeless Tobacco in the Western World* (New York: Praeger).

Rubin, R., Charron, C. and Dorsey, M. (2001), *Online Tobacco Sales Grow, States Lose* (Cambridge, MA: Forrester Research Inc.).

Saba, R., Beard, T.R., Ekelund, R.B. and Ressler, R.W. (1995), "The Demand for Cigarette Smuggling", *Economic Inquiry*, **33**, 189–202.

Saffer, H. and Chaloupka, F. (1999), *Tobacco Advertising: Economic Theory and International Evidence*, (NBER working paper 6958).

Saffer, H. and Chaloupka, F. (2000), "The Effect of Tobacco Advertising Bans on Tobacco Consumption", *Journal of Health Economics*, **19**, 1117–1137. [PubMed 11186847] [DOI: 10.1016/S0167–6296%2800%2900054–0].

Schmalensee, R. (1972), *The Economics of Advertising* (Amsterdam: North-Holland).

Seiglie, C. (1990), "A Theory of the Politically Optimal Commodity Tax", *Economic Inquiry*, **28**, 586–603.

Seldon, B. and Doroodian, K. (1989), "A Simultaneous Model of Cigarette Advertising: Effects on Demand and Industry Response to Public Policy", *Review of Economics and Statistics*, **71**, 673–677. [DOI: 10.2307/1928110].

Simon, J.L. (1966), "The Price Elasticity of Liquor in the U.S., and a Simple Method of Determination", *Econometrica*, **34**, 193–205. [DOI: 10.2307/1909863].

Sloan, F.A. and Trogdon, J.G. (2004), "The Impact of the Master Settlement Agreement on Cigarette Consumption", *Journal of Policy Analysis and Management*, **23**, 843–855. [PubMed 15499706] [DOI: 10.1002/pam.20050].

Statistics Canada (1999), *Smoking Behaviour of Canadians*, www.hc-sc.gc.ca/hpb/lcdc/bc/nphs/nphs12_e.html.

Stavrinos, V.G. (1987), "The Effects of an Anti-Smoking Campaign on Cigarette Consumption: Empirical Evidence from Greece", *Applied Economics*, **19**, 323–329.

Stephens, T., Pederson, L.L., Koval, J.J. and Kim, C. (1997), "The Relationship of Cigarette Prices and No-Smoking Bylaws to the Prevalence of Smoking in Canada", *American Journal of Public Health*, **87**, 1519–1521. [PubMed 9314807].

Stewart, M.J. (1993), "The Effect on Tobacco Consumption of Advertising Bans in OECD Countries", *International Journal of Advertising*, **12**, 155–180.

Sung, H.Y., Hu, T.W., and Keeler, T.E. (1994), "Cigarette Taxation and Demand: An Empirical Model", *Contemporary Economic Policy*, **12**, 91–100.

Sweanor, D.T. and Martial, L.R. (1994), *The Smuggling of Tobacco Products: Lessons from Canada* (Ottawa, Ontario: Non-Smokers), Rights Association/Smoking and Health Action Foundation.

Tansel, A. (1993), "Cigarette Demand, Health Scares and Education in Turkey", *Applied Economics*, **25**, 521–529.

Tauras, J.A. and Chaloupka, F.J. (2003), "The Demand for Nicotine Replacement Therapies", *Nicotine and Tobacco Research*, **5**, 237–243. [PubMed 12745497] [DOI: 10.1080/1462220031000073306].

Tauras, J.A., Chaloupka, F.J. and Emery, S.L. (2003), "Nicotine Replacement Therapy Demand: The Impact of Prices and Advertising". Working Paper (Department of Economics, University of Illinois at Chicago).

Tegene, A. (1991), "Kalman Filter and the Demand for Cigarettes", *Applied Economics*, **23**, 1175–1182.

Thursby, J.G. and Thursby, M.C. (2000), "Interstate Cigarette Bootlegging: Extent, Revenue Losses, and Effects of Federal Intervention", *National Tax Journal*, **53**, 59–78.

Thursby, M., Jensen, R. and Thursby, J. (1991), "Smuggling, Camouflaging, and Market Structure", *Quarterly Journal of Economics*, **106**, 789–814. [DOI: 10.2307/2937927].

Townsend, J., Roderick, P. and Cooper, J. (1994), "Cigarette Smoking by Socio Economic Group, Sex, and Age: Effects of Price, Income, and Health Publicity", *British Medical Journal*, **309**, 923–927. [PubMed 7950662].

Townsend, J.L. (1987), "Cigarette Tax, Economic Welfare, and Social Class Patterns of Smoking", *Applied Economics*, **19**, 355–365.

Tremblay, C.H. and Tremblay, V.J. (1995), "The Impact of Cigarette Advertising on Consumer Surplus, Profit, and Social Welfare", *Contemporary Economic Policy*, **13**, 113–124.

Tremblay, C.H. and Tremblay, V.J. (1999), "Reinterpreting the Effect of an Advertising Ban on Cigarette Smoking", *International Journal of Advertising*, **18**, 41–50.

U.S. Department of Health and Human Services (2000), *Reducing Tobacco Use: A Report of the Surgeon General* (Atlanta, GA: Centers for Disease Control and Prevention).

U.S. General Accounting Office (2001), *Tobacco Settlement: States' Use of Master Settlement Agreement Payments*. Washington: USGPO.

UICC (1996), *Cigarette Smuggling*, UICC Tobacco Control Fact Sheet No. 13. www.globalink.org/tobacco/fact_sheets/13fact.htm.

United States Department of Agriculture (2002), *Foreign Agricultural Service, Tobacco: World Markets and Trade.* (Circular Series FT–3–02).

U.S. Census Bureau (various years), *Statistical Abstract of the United States* Washington, DC: U.S. Government Printing Office).

U.S. Public Health Service, *The Surgeon General's Report on Reducing Tobacco Use Warning Label Fact Sheet.* www.tobaccowall.ucsf.edu/pdf.warninglabel.pdf.

Valdes, B. (1993), "Cigarette Consumption in Spain: Empirical Evidence and Implications for Public Health Policy", *Applied Economics*, **25**, 149–156.

Viscusi, W.K. (1993), "Cigarette Warnings: The Perils of the Cipollone Decision", *Supreme Court Economic Review*, **2**, 239–275.

Viscusi, W.K. (1995), "Cigarette Taxation and the Social Consequences of Smoking", in *Tax Policy and the Economy*, Poterba, J. (ed.) (Cambridge, MA: MIT Press), 51–101.

Viscusi, W.K. (2002), *Smoke-Filled Rooms: A Postmortem on the Tobacco Deal* (Chicago: University of Chicago Press).

Wakefield, M. and Chaloupka, F. (2000), "Effectiveness of Comprehensive Tobacco Control Programmes in Reducing Teenage Smoking in the USA", *Tobacco Control*, **9**, 177–186. [PubMed 10841854] [DOI: 10.1136/tc.9.2.177].

Wakefield, M.A., Wilson, D., Owen, N., Esterman, A. and Roberts, L. (1992), "Workplace Smoking Restrictions, Occupational Status, and Reduced Cigarette Consumption", *Journal of Occupational Medicine*, **34**, 693–697. [PubMed 1494961].

Warner, K.E. (1982), "Cigarette Excise Taxation and Interstate Smuggling: An Assessment of Recent Activity", *National Tax Journal*, **35**(4), 438–490.

Warner, K.E. (1990), "Tobacco Taxation as Health Policy in the Third World", *American Journal of Public Health*, **80**, 529–531. [PubMed 2327526].

Wasserman, J., Manning, W., Newhouse, J. and Winkler, J. (1991), "The Effects of Excise Taxes and Regulations on Cigarette Smoking", *Journal of Health Economics*, **10**, 43–64. [PubMed 10112149] [DOI: 10.1016/0167–6296%2891%2990016–G].

Wilcox, G.B., Tharp, M. and Yang, K.T. (1994), "Cigarette Advertising and Consumption in South Korea, 1988-1992", *International Journal of Advertising*, **13**, 333–346.

Wilson, J.J. (1999), *Summary of the Attorneys General Master Tobacco Settlement Agreement. Washington*, Vol. DC (National Conference of State Legislators), http://www.ncsl.org/statefed/tmsasumm.htm.

Winer, S.L. and Hettich, W. (1991), "Debt and Tariffs: An Empirical Investigation of the Evolution of Revenue Systems", *Journal of Public Economics*, **45**, 215–242. [DOI: 10.1016/0047-2727%2891%2990040-9].

Witt, S.F. and Pass, C.L. (1981), "The Effects of Health Warnings and Advertising on the Demand for Cigarettes", *Scottish Journal of Political Economy*, **28**, 86–91.

Woollery, T., Asma, S. and Sharp, D. (2000), "Clean Indoor-Air Laws and Youth Access Restrictions", in *Tobacco Control in Developing Countries*, Jha, P. and Chaloupka, F.J. (eds) (London: Oxford University Press), 273–286.

World Bank (1999), "Curbing the Epidemic: Governments and the Economics of Tobacco Control", www1.worldbank.org/tobacco/reports_pdf.htm.

World Health Organization (WHO) (1996), The Tobacco Epidemic: A Global Public Health Emergency, Fact Sheet No. 118, www.who.int/inf-fs/en/fact118.html; www.who.int/archives/tohalert/apr96/intro.htm.

World Health Organization (WHO) (2003), "An International Treaty for Tobacco Control", http://www.who.int/features/2003/08/en/print.html.

Yorozu, I. and Zhou, J.Y. (2004), "Negative Externality, Tacit Bargaining and Cigarette Demand: The Case of Environmental Tobacco Smoke in Japan" in *Progress in Economics Research*, Tavidze, A. (ed.), 91–107.

Young, T. (1983), "The Demand for Cigarettes: Alternative Specifications of Fujii's Model", *Applied Economics*, **15**, 203–211.

Yurekli, A.A. and Zhang, P. (2000), "The Impact of Clean Indoor-Air Laws and Cigarette Smuggling on Demand for Cigarettes: An Empirical Model", *Health Economics*, **9**, 159–170. [PubMed 10721017] [DOI: 10.1002/%28SICI%291099-1050%28200003%299%3A2%3C159%3A%3AAID-HEC499%3E3.0.CO%3B2-T].

Zanias, G.P. (1987), "The Demand for Cigarettes: Habit Formation and Health Scare", *Greek Economic Review*, **17**, 248–262.

Zweifel, F. (2001), "Improved Risk Information, the Demand for Cigarettes, and Anti-Tobacco Policy", *The Journal of Risk and Uncertainty*, **23**(3), 299–303. [DOI: 10.1023/A%3A1011829925205].

Index

Printed in the United States
by Baker & Taylor Publisher Services